PROPHETS AND WISE MEN

STUDIES IN BIBLICAL THEOLOGY

PROPHETS AND WISE MEN

WILLIAM McKANE

WIPF & STOCK · Eugene, Oregon

Wipf and Stock Publishers
199 W 8th Ave, Suite 3
Eugene, OR 97401

Prophets and Wise Men
By McKane, William

ISBN 13: 978-1-60899-030-6
Publication date 9/25/2009
Previously published by SCM Press, 1965

First English edition 1965 by SCM Press
This Edition published by arrangement with SCM-Canterbury Press

CONTENTS

PREFACE

THERE are passages in the prophetic books of the Old Testament in which the statesmanship of Israel's wise men comes under fire. The book originates in this simple observation and its purpose is to explore and explain the causes of this tension and incompatibility between prophet and statesman. Since the arguments employed incorporate a fair weight of detail, the book will in places present a rather complicated appearance to the reader. This will be the case particularly with Part One, for the role of the prophet is generally better known and understood than the aspect of wisdom which is there expounded.

The intention of Part One is to introduce the reader to these wise men and their world. They have to be viewed and understood in their habitat, if the core of their conflict with the prophets is to be probed and laid bare. In this way the foundations are laid for Part Two, which is essentially simple in its conception and in which the passages dealing with the conflict between prophets and wise men are individually examined. The enhanced understanding of these wise men carried over from Part One will then throw new light on the subject-matter of Part Two. The results of the enquiry are finally stated in a conclusion which gathers together the preceding arguments, but which concentrates on the broad implications of the conflict and is intended to ensure against the danger of not seeing the wood for the trees.

The object of the exercise is not to take sides with either statesman or prophet. Partisanship will not do justice to this conflict nor show its contemporary relevance. On the other hand, it is not enough to 'explain' the conflict from a position of neutrality or assumed superiority. The mere spectator will not understand it at its deeper levels. Ultimately the ground of our understanding must be our participation in a similar conflict; these tensions and incompatibilities are facts of our existence and prophet and statesman still confront each other with arguments the same in all essentials.

The University,
Glasgow

WILLIAM MCKANE

ABBREVIATIONS

AASOR	*Annual of the American Schools of Oriental Research*
ATD	Das Alte Testament Deutsch
BASOR	*Bulletin of the American Schools of Oriental Research*
BH	*Biblia Hebraica*[4], ed. R. Kittel and P. Kahle
BWANT	Beiträge zur Wissenschaft vom Alten und Neuen Testament
BZAW	Beihefte zur *Zeitschrift für die alttestamentliche Wissenschaft*
G.	Greek version of the Old Testament (Septuagint)
HAT	Handbuch zum Alten Testament
HKAT	Handkommentar zum Alten Testament
ICC	The International Critical Commentary
JBL	*Journal of Biblical Literature*
JEA	*Journal of Egyptian Archaeology*
JSS	*Journal of Semitic Studies*
KAT	Kommentar zum Alten Testament
KHKAT	Kurzer Handkommentar zum Alten Testament
MT	Masoretic Text
PEQ	*Palestine Exploration Quarterly*
RA	*Revue d'Assyriologie*
RB	*Revue Biblique*
S.	Syriac version of the Old Testament (Peshitta)
SJT	*Scottish Journal of Theology*
T.	Targum
TLZ	*Theologische Literaturzeitung*
VT	*Vetus Testamentum*
ZAW	*Zeitschrift für die alttestamentliche Wissenschaft*

Note: Biblical references give chapter and verse of the Hebrew Bible. Those of the English versions, where they differ, follow in square brackets.

PART ONE

OLD WISDOM
AND THE CASE OF AHITHOPHEL

INTRODUCTORY

We read concerning Ahithophel in II Sam. 16.23: 'And the advice (*'ēṣā*) of Ahithophel which he gave in those days was as if (*ka'ašer*) one should ask concerning the word (*dāḇār*) of God. Thus was all the advice which Ahithophel gave both to David and Absalom.'

Scott[1] says that the meaning of this is that the *'ēṣā* of Ahithophel had almost but not quite the status of the *dāḇār* of God, but we can conclude no more from the grammar (*ka'ašer*) than that the relationship between *'ēṣā* and *dāḇār* is one of equivalence or approximate equivalence. Von Rad's remarks[2] on the non-authoritarian character of *'ēṣā* as opposed to the imperative of the revealed *dāḇār* of God suggest another exegesis for this verse, namely, the *'ēṣā* of Ahithophel was so compelling that it was more mandatory than advice; it demanded acceptance and, in assuming this authoritative character, it approximated to the binding word of God.

In any case the verse points to the influential role of wisdom in matters of state and the reputation enjoyed by its leading exponents, for the words 'Thus was all the advice which Ahithophel gave both to David and Absalom' establish this connection between *'ēṣā* and political advice or policy. There are two tasks which this verse invites us to undertake. The first is the general elucidation of the political role of old wisdom and the second a consideration of the respective spheres of *'ēṣā* and *dāḇār* in the Old Testament in relation to statesmanship and political decisions. The phrasing of the verse suggests that they constitute two alternative and disconnected systems of political guidance, but this is at best a provisional definition or working arrangement and it discloses a situation in which the seeds of conflict are present.

[1] R. B. Y. Scott, 'Priesthood, Prophecy, Wisdom and the Knowledge of God', *JBL* 80 (1961), p. 3.

[2] G. von Rad, 'Die ältere Weisheit Israels', *Kerygma und Dogma* 2 (1956), p. 64. W. Zimmerli, 'Zur Struktur der alttestamentlichen Weisheit', *ZAW* 10 (1933), p. 181, makes a similar distinction between *'ēṣā* and *miṣwā*. Cf. J. Fichtner, 'Jesaja unter den Weisen', *TLZ* 74 (1949), col. 75.

I

WISDOM AND STATESMANSHIP

It has often been pointed out that there is a strain of wisdom in the Old Testament which is this-worldly and has no commitment to ethical values, and it has usually been assumed that this brand of wisdom was subsequently transformed through its subjection to distinctively Israelite religious and ethical insights.[1] The range of meaning covered by √*ḥkm* in biblical Hebrew is considerable. Its use in connection with technical skill and manual dexterity is well attested[2] and there are two points about these passages which deserve comment. First the phrase *ḥaḵᵉmē lēḇ* used of the craftsmen in Ex. 28.3 (cf. *ḥaḵᵉmaṯ lēḇ* in 35.25). This use of *lēḇ* in the context of craftsmanship is a reminder that 'mind' is sometimes a better translation of this word than 'heart'. Here, where it refers to technical skill and craftsmanship, *lēḇ* has no emotional associations (it is not a warm word).

Lēḇ has close associations with the ethos of old wisdom and a word similarly connected is *bīnā* ('perspicacity'). *Bīnā* is often used of the penetration and clarity of thought which are desiderated in a man of affairs, but in II Chron. 2.12 Huramabi, a master craftsman, is described as a wise man who knows perspicacity (*bīnā*). Here it is associated with the insight and clarity of purpose of a craftsman.

[1] So H. Gressmann, 'Die neugefundene Lehre des Amenemope und die vorexilische Spruchdichtung Israels', *ZAW* 41 (1924), pp. 289–91. J. Fichtner, *Die altorientalische Weisheit in ihrer israelitischjüdischen Ausprägung* (BZAW 62, 1933), pp. 13–59. W. Baumgartner, *Israelitische und altorientalische Weisheit* (1933), pp. 4–5. W. Zimmerli, *op. cit.*, p. 180. H. L. Jansen, *Die spätjüdische Psalmendichtung. Ihr Entstehungskreis und ihr 'Sitz im Leben'* (1937), p. 57. H. Duesberg, *Les scribes inspirés*, i (1938–9), p. 240. R. H. Pfeiffer, *Introduction to the Old Testament* (1941), pp. 650ff. G. Östborn, *Tōrā in the Old Testament* (1945), p. 122. H. H. Cazelles, 'A propos d'une phrase de H. H. Rowley', *Wisdom in Israel and the Ancient Near East* (*Supplement to VT* III, Rowley Festschrift, edited by M. Noth and D. W. Thomas, 1955), pp. 26–31. M. Noth, 'Die Bewährung von Salomos "Göttlicher Weisheit"' (Rowley Festschrift), p. 232. Cf. G. von Rad, 'Die ältere Weisheit Israels', p. 69, n. 40.

[2] Ex. 28.3; 35.25; 36.4; Isa. 40.20; Jer. 10.9; Ezek. 27.8–9; I Chron. 22.15; II Chron. 2.6 [7], 12. In Ezek. 27.8 *ḥᵃḵāmayiḵ ṣōr* should perhaps be emended to *ḥaḵᵉmē ṣemer* (so *BH*), 'skilled men of Ṣemer'. In any case the reference is to navigational skill (*ḥōḇᵉlāyiḵ* means 'pilots' or 'navigators'). In v. 9 *ḥᵃḵāmēhā* refers to those skilled in ship repairing, perhaps in the caulking of seams.

The second point which I would make in connection with these passages is that in Ex. 28.3 the skill of the craftsman is not portrayed in terms of native endowment; it is not the result of a period of rigorous apprenticeship, but is rather the gift of Yahweh who has filled the *ḥaḵᵉmē lēḇ* with the spirit (*rūaḥ*) of wisdom. This represents one aspect of the accommodation of the vocabulary of old wisdom to Israelite piety.[1]

Two passages illustrate particularly well the lack of ethical commitment in this old wisdom. In II Sam. 13.3 Jonadab is described as a wise man and it is evident that in this context *ḥāḵām* has no moralizing tendency. All that is meant is that Jonadab's plan is shrewd in its conception and well adapted to enable Amnon to satisfy his desire. In this respect the plan is the work of a *ḥāḵām* and the fact that Jonadab uses his wisdom to secure an immoral end is not thought to impair its validity, since there is no element of ethical evaluation in the meaning. In other words √*ḥkm* refers here only to competence and efficiency—to the ability to devise a plan which will work.[2]

In I Kings 2 we have what I take to be a mixture of piety and old wisdom,[3] but for the moment I deal only with vv. 5–9, where considerations of political expediency prevail. In v. 6 David says to Solomon: 'Act according to your wisdom (*ḥoḵmā*), but do not let his (Joab's) head go down to Sheol in peace.' Again in v. 9: 'You are a wise man (*ḥāḵām*) and you know what to do with him (Shimei).' In both instances David is advising Solomon to assassinate men who, in his judgment, have become too bad political risks to be allowed to live, and he tells Solomon that he will have to use his own judgment and shrewdness as to the best time to strike and the means which will have the least unfavourable repercussions on the stability of his kingdom. The ethical indifference or neutrality of √*ḥkm* is thus unmistakable. The same can also be demonstrated for √*śkl* in Dan. 8.25, where it is said of Antiochus Epiphanes that by his aptitude (*śeḵel*) he will make *mirmā* ('deceit' or 'intrigue') to prosper in his hand.

It has often been noted that this hard-headed wisdom is international, that it is specially orientated towards the arts of govern-

[1] See below, pp. 86ff.
[2] *nitḥakkᵉmā* is similarly used in Ex. 1.10.
[3] See below, pp. 108–9.

ment and that it has a close affinity with political and administrative aptitudes.[1] It is empirical in its spirit, with an emphasis on intellectual rather than ethical values and so well adapted to the hard realities of statecraft and government. Its practitioners were therefore pre-eminently an *élite* who were in the higher echelons of government and administration and we shall see that the literature of this wisdom was directed particularly towards the training of statesmen, diplomats and administrators in the schools whose educational discipline was shaped to this end.[2]

The title of 'Scribe' was given to such high officials in Egypt and that of 'Scribe' or 'Secretary' to their counterparts in Babylonia and Assyria. Ahikar, who is represented as an Assyrian official and whose Assyrian origins do not seem to be in doubt,[3] is named 'a sagacious and ready Secretary' (*spr ḥkym wmhyr*).[4] He is also 'counsellor' of all Assyria and bearer of the seal on whose advice (*ʿṭh*) Sennacherib, King of Assyria, leans.[5] The same technical sense of 'Scribe' or 'Secretary' is attested for the Old Testament as the following passages show.

II Sam. 8.16–18 (20.23–25) is an official list of the leading members of David's establishment, ecclesiastical, civil and military.[6] The two political officials mentioned are Jehoshaphat who is *mazkīr* and Seraiah[7] who is *sōpēr*. However these two terms are translated there is no doubt that Seraiah is a 'Scribe' or 'Secretary' of the same kind as Ahikar[8] and that both Jehoshaphat and Seraiah are officials of the highest rank.[9]

I Chron. 27.32–34 gives us information about certain other high officials of David. Both Jonathan, the uncle of David, and Ahithophel have the title 'Counsellor' (*yōʿēṣ*), but whereas Ahithophel is the 'King's Counsellor', Jonathan along with Jehiel is a 'Counsellor' to the king's sons. Hushai occupies another key

[1] H. Duesberg, *op. cit.*, i, p. 240. W. Baumgartner, 'The Wisdom Literature', *The Old Testament and Modern Study* (edited by H. H. Rowley, 1951), pp. 211–14. G. von Rad, 'Die ältere Weisheit Israels', pp. 62–63.

[2] See below, pp. 36ff.

[3] See below, pp. 28ff.

[4] A. E. Cowley, *Aramaic Papyri of the Fifth Century BC* (1923), pp. 210ff., *Ahikar* 1.1. Cf. 1.12, 'the wise Secretary' (*sprʾ ḥkymʾ*). Also 1.28, *spr ḥkym*; cf. 3.35.

[5] *Ahikar* 1.3, 4, 7, 12; 2.17; 3.35–36, 42–43; 4.55, 61.

[6] Parallel to I Sam. 8.16–18 is I Chron. 18.15–17.

[7] See below, p. 27, n. 4.

[8] So W. Baumgartner, *Israelitische und altorientalische Weisheit*, p. 20.

[9] So J. Begrich, 'Sōfēr und Mazkīr', *ZAW* 58 (1940–1), p. 3.

advisory office—he is the 'King's Friend' (*rēaʿhammelek̠*),[1] the post held by Zabud during Solomon's reign (I Kings 4.5). Jonathan is credited with one of the fundamental intellectual virtues of the professional political adviser in that he is perspicacious or 'a man of insight' (*'îš mēḇîn*). According to MT but not G.[B] he was a *sōp̄ēr* as well as a *yōʿēṣ*, but it is unlikely that this refers to his tenancy of the particular high political office mentioned in the other official lists (II Sam. 8.17; 20.25; I Kings 4.3). Rather he is a 'Secretary' in the more general sense that he belongs to a professional class whose members are distinguished by their mental habits and who serve in high places in the government and administration.

This passage might be thought to lend some credence to the conclusion that a *yōʿēṣ* is not necessarily a *sōp̄ēr*, since otherwise there is no particular point in noting that Jonathan is both a *yōʿēṣ* and a *sōp̄ēr*. Even if the text is to be relied upon in this particular, I do not believe that this would be a safe conclusion, and this passage does not seem to me to throw any light on the precise nature of the relationship between *sōp̄ēr* and *yōʿēs* or between *sōp̄ēr* and *ḥāḵām*.[2] This is a matter which I shall take up presently, but it will be sufficient for the moment to notice that the testimony of this list that Ahithophel and Hushai were leading statesmen in the reign of David is supported by the influential role which both play as policy-makers in the Ahithophel-Absalom story (II Sam. 15–17).

I Kings 4.1–6 contains a list of Solomon's chief officials and all of them, civil, military and ecclesiastical, are called *śārîm*. The hereditary principle is seen to apply both in the civil and ecclesiastical spheres. Azariah is son of Zadok and the office of Secretary which had been held by Seraiah[3] appears to be held jointly by his two sons.[4] Jehoshaphat is still *mazkîr* and the office of King's

[1] Perhaps, however, rather than an office this is an honorific title such as would be bestowed by the king on a minister of the first rank. See especially W. A. Ward, 'The Egyptian Office of Joseph', *JSS* 5 (1960), p. 147. Cf. the title 'Father to Pharaoh' given to Joseph (Gen. 45.8). See W. A. Ward, *ibid.*, p. 149.

[2] See below, pp. 23ff.

[3] See below, p. 27, n. 4.

[4] Cf. J. Begrich, 'Sōfēr und Mazkir', p. 8. Begrich suggests that the two sons were perhaps not in office at the same time. K. Galling, 'Die israelitische Staatsverfassung in ihrer vorderorientalischen Umwelt', *Der Alte Orient* 28 (1929), p. 39, thinks that the names Elihoreph and Ahijah are Egyptian and Babylonian respectively and that this points to the bilingual diplomatic correspondence which had to be managed (see below, pp. 27ff.).

Friend which had been held in David's reign by Hushai is now occupied by Zabud, who is also said to be a priest—perhaps an indication that the ecclesiastical establishment could also be politically influential[1] (cf. II Kings 19.2, Isa. 37.2, where Eliakim and Shebna, two leading members of the political establishment, are accompanied by senior priests on their mission to Isaiah).

This list is larger than those coming from David's reign and this may be a pointer to the more complicated structure of Solomon's bureaucracy.[2] Azariah, the son of Nathan, is in charge of the *niṣṣāḇîm*—no doubt the twelve officials appointed by Solomon over all Israel (I Kings 4.7), each of whom was responsible for the provisioning of the royal household for one month of the year. Ahishar, who is 'over the House' (*'al habbayiṯ*), holds an office which is mentioned again in the reign of Hezekiah (II Kings 18.18; Isa. 36.3).[3] The statement that Azariah, the son of Zadok, was 'the priest' (*hakkōhēn*) would seem to indicate that he had succeeded to the office which his father had held jointly with Abiathar, but these two are still designated 'priests' in v. 4. Does this mean that Zadok and Abiathar had been passed over for Azariah? Or have we here a list which gives us the holders of the office at different periods in Solomon's reign? That is to say, Zadok and Abiathar were succeeded by Azariah.

In Kings 12.11 [10] mention is made of a 'Royal Secretary' (*sōp̄ēr hammeleḵ*)[4] who acted with the high priest in counting and removing the money which was collected in a box for the fabric fund of the temple. This Royal Secretary should probably be equated with the *sōp̄ēr* of II Sam. 8.17 and 20.25 and so is Joash's Secretary of State. This probability is increased by the circumstance that Shaphan who certainly held this office once acted in a similar capacity and was sent to Hilkiah, the high priest, in order to find out how much money was in the temple fabric fund (II Kings 22.3ff.; cf. II Chron. 24.11, according to which it was the officer (*pāqîḏ*) of the high priest and not that dignitary himself who was involved in this particular duty).

The role of the 'Secretary' here may be an illustration of the overlapping of the functions of the civil and ecclesiastical

[1] See below.
[2] Cf. H. Duesberg, *op. cit.*, i, pp. 201ff.
[3] See below, p. 20.
[4] See below, p. 24.

establishments.[1] Begrich[2] holds that it was within the competence of the 'Secretary' to enquire at the oracle of the state God in time of distress, a statement which he bases on Isa. 37.1ff. Here the leading royal officials certainly seek an interview with Isaiah, but it is not clear that they are asking his advice. It appears rather that he volunteers a prophecy to them. Verse 4 is obscure and v. 5 does not agree with the representation of the preceding verses. According to v. 5 the officials of Hezekiah do not speak, while vv. 3–4 have it that they ask Isaiah to pray for the remnant which was left. Thus while they appear to have been asking the prophet to fulfil his role as an intercessor, there is no evidence in the passage that their intention was to consult the oracle.

The offices mentioned in II Kings 18.18 (Isa. 36.3) are already familiar to us from the previous lists. Shebna is *hassōpēr* and Joah *hammazkīr*. Eliakim is *'ašer 'al habbayiṯ*[3] and *bayiṯ* is certainly the palace and not the temple, but otherwise we can no more define the precise functions of this office than we can do in the case of the other two. We can, however, perhaps conclude that these three were the king's leading advisers and together constituted the inner circle of government. The name of Eliakim occurs first and it has been assumed that this points to his precedence over the other two, but it is unwise to read so much into the order of this list (cf. I Kings 4.6, where *'al habbayiṯ* occurs near the end of the list).

Begrich[4] argues that the *sōpēr* takes precedence over the *mazkīr* and that the precedence of the *mazkīr* in the lists referring to David's reign is to be accounted for in two ways: by the erroneous transmission of the list in II Sam. 8.16–18 which has influenced the form of 20.23–25 and by the circumstance that the *sōpēr* in these lists is a foreigner over whom the *mazkīr*, as the son of an Israelite, has been given precedence. Concerning *'al habbayiṯ*, Begrich says that by the time of Isaiah the enhancement of this office is complete and that it takes precedence over the other two. He claims that it is evident from Isa. 22.20ff. that *'ašer 'al habbayiṯ* had all the powers of a vizier in his hand.[5] But from this period onwards, according to

[1] Cf. H. Duesberg, *op. cit.*, i, p. 4.
[2] J. Begrich, 'Sōfēr und Mazkīr', p. 4.
[3] For comparable Babylonian and Assyrian offices see B. Meissner, *Babylonien und Assyrien* (1920), i, pp. 118, 131.
[4] J. Begrich, *op. cit.*, pp. 5–9.
[5] Similarly R. de Vaux, 'Titres et fonctionnaires égyptiens à la cour de David et de Solomon', *RB* 48 (1939), pp. 401–3. G. von Rad, *Genesis* (tr. J. H. Marks, 1961), p. 372.

Begrich, the office entered a period of decline and by the time of Jeremiah (36) the *sōpēr* had re-established the primacy of his office. Ward[1] equates 'you shall be over my house' (Gen. 41.40) with such Egyptian titles as 'Great Steward of the Two Lands' and 'Great Chief in the Palace' and argues that Joseph did not hold the office of vizier. His conclusion is that Joseph, as *'ašer 'al habbayiṯ* and Minister of Agriculture and as the holder of several honorific titles which mark him out as a foremost adviser of Pharaoh, was a leading and influential statesman but not the vizier.

It is clear that *hassōpēr* of Jer. 36.11ff. is one of the statesmen (*śārīm*) and that the 'cabinet meeting' takes place in his room.[2] He is therefore to be identified with *hassōpēr* of the lists and he seems to act here as the king's first minister. Since *hassōpēr* in Jer. 37.15 is also associated with the *śārīm*, it is reasonable to suppose that he is the holder of the same office and this conclusion is supported by the circumstance that Jeremiah is imprisoned in his house, for it is unlikely that the *śārīm* would select the house of a run-of-the-mill 'writer'[3] to confine a dangerous political prisoner. The only difficulty of this interpretation is the assumption which it requires that the office of *hassōpēr* has changed hands in the interval. In 36.11ff. the occupant is Elishama, while in 37.15ff. it is held by Jonathan.

Finally there is the 'Secretary' (*sāpᵉrā*) of Ezra 4.8, 9, 17, 23, who wrote to Artaxerxes on behalf of those who had been settled in Samaria and the province Beyond the River. This Shimshai is a colleague (*kᵉnōṯ*)[4] of leading officials, including the chief government officer (*bᵉ'ēl ṭᵉ'ēm*).[5] Hence Shimshai is a high civil servant—a Secretary with a capital S.[6]

There are also one or two cases in the Old Testament where *sōpēr* is apparently the title of an official with military functions. Gressmann[7] translates Jer. 52.25 (*sōpēr śar haṣṣāḇā'*) 'The Secretary

[1] W. A. Ward, *op. cit.*, pp. 144–50.

[2] *Liškā* (v. 12), see below, p. 122.

[3] See below, pp. 23ff.

[4] W. Baumgartner, *Lexicon in Veteris Testamenti Libros* (1958), *s.v. kᵉnōṯ*.

[5] W. Baumgartner, *ibid,. s.v. ṭᵉ'ēm*.

[6] So H. H. Schaeder, *Esra der Schreiber* (1930), p. 41. Schaeder notes that *sāpᵉrā* appears before the Persian period in Babylonian Aramaic with the meaning of 'Secretary' and he cites from the Elephantine Papyri (A. E. Cowley, *op. cit.*, pp. 4, 53). Since the Persian kings used imperial Aramaic as the language of diplomacy, they retained *sāpᵉrā* as the designation of an official, and the same terminology transposed into Hebrew is used by Nehemiah in his memorandum (*hassōpēr*, Neh. 13.13).

[7] H. Gressmann, 'Die neugefundene Lehre des Amenemope und die vorexilische Spruchdichtung Israels', p. 293.

of the Field Marshal'. The Hebrew of the parallel passage, however, is *hassōp̄ēr śar haṣṣāḇā'* (II Kings 25.19) and this has to be translated 'The Secretary, Commander of the Army', which could be paraphrased as 'Secretary of State for War'. It is stated in both passages that the *sōp̄ēr* was responsible for levying the people for military service and he is mentioned in company with several others who were considered by Nebuchudrezzar sufficiently influential to be singled out for deportation. Among these were the principal ecclesiastics,[1] a military officer and five (seven according to Jer. 52.25) leading advisers of the king.[2]

Sōp̄ēr also appears in the Song of Deborah (Judg. 5.14) as the title of a military official and the *šēḇeṭ* of this *sōp̄ēr* is evidently a symbol of his authority. We must conclude in this case that either he is responsible for mobilization or that he is a high-ranking military officer. The parallel word in this verse (*mᵉḥōqēq*) appears elsewhere in the Old Testament with the meaning 'staff', but its literal translation would be 'inscriber' or 'one who promulgates a decree' which would tend to support the conclusion that this is an official who is responsible for the muster.[3]

[1] The 'Keepers of the Threshold' (*šōmᵉrē hassap̄*) are also mentioned in II Kings 12.10 [9] and 22.4, besides the parallel passage to Jer. 52.24, which is II Kings 25.18. These were senior members of the ecclesiastical establishment. See W. McKane, 'A Note on II Kings 12.10', *ZAW* 71 (1959), pp. 260–5.

[2] Literally: 'Five (or "seven") of those who see the face of the king.' Cf. Esth. 1.14, where the number of those who see the face of the Persian king is seven. They are designated *śārīm* and are said to sit first in the kingdom. They are thus the inner circle of the king's political advisers and it is one of the seven (Memucan) who speaks and offers advice (*ʿēṣā*) to the king.

[3] The passage is obscure. RSV: 'From Machir marched down the commanders and from Zebulon those who bear the marshal's staff.' Perhaps rather 'those who grasp (√*mšk*) the baton of a *sōp̄ēr*'. *BH*: 'Those who grasp the baton' (*sōp̄ēr* perhaps a gloss).

II

WRITING AND STATESMANSHIP

I COME now to a closer consideration of the relationship between the title *sōpēr* as applied to a high official and the mastery of writing. I take as a point of departure a statement made by Nielsen: 'The political central administration would not dispense with writing. From the time of David one or more *sōpherīm* make their appearance at the royal courts, but these are evidently high officials and not merely clerks.'[1] There is no doubt, as we shall see,[2] that in the Old Testament *sōpēr* can mean 'writer' or 'clerk' (in the modern, not the medieval, sense), and it is equally clear that the word has a technical or specialized meaning best conveyed by our *Secretary*[3] in such compounds as Secretary of State, Foreign Secretary, Home Secretary, and so on. The problem is to determine to what extent the idea of 'writing' enters into the title 'Secretary'. I shall argue that the translation 'Scribe' is usually taken to indicate a more intrinsic connection between the office of 'Secretary' and 'writing' or 'correspondence' than really exists.

It has been argued that during the reigns of David and Solomon Israel was in the Egyptian rather than the Babylonian sphere of influence, that there is evidence of close relations between Solomon and Egypt and that we ought to seek there for the models of Solomon's bureaucracy.[4] I do not doubt that there is a great deal in this argument, but I have no knowledge of Egyptology and so I am unable to assess precisely how successful Begrich[5] has been

[1] Edouard Nielsen, *Oral Tradition* (1954), p. 43.

[2] See below, pp. 33ff.

[3] So B. Gemser, *Sprüche Salomos* (HAT, 1937), p. 2. A. Bentzen, *Introduction to the Old Testament* [5] (1959), i, pp. 170–1.

[4] So W. Baumgartner, *Israelitische und altorientalische Weisheit*, p. 13. J. Begrich, *op. cit.*, pp. 10–13. R. de Vaux, *op. cit.*, p. 395.

[5] There is one part of Begrich's argument which I find particularly unconvincing. He urges (*ibid.*, p. 15, n. 1) that *śar* and *śārīm* always occur in the construct relationship in the period prior to Solomon, with an absolute defining the area of responsibility (Judg. 9.30; II Sam. 24.2), and that the absolute use of *śārīm* with the meaning 'high royal officials' is to be traced to the influence of *Egyptian śr w* which is a technical term for high royal officials.

in his attempt to find an Egyptian model for the Israelite office of *sōpēr*. But in any case 'Scribe' is a title which is applied in Egypt to any official and this usage can give no precise indication of the content of his office. The manner in which the idea of 'writing' enters into the Egyptian title of 'Scribe' has been correctly stated by Erman:

'Through the Egyptian people from the earliest period there ran a deep cleavage which separated him who had enjoyed a higher education from the common mass. It came into existence when the Egyptians had invented their writing, for he who mastered it, however humble his position might outwardly be, at once gained a superiority over his fellows. Without the assistance of his scribes even the ruler was of no account and it was not without good reason that the high officials of the Old Kingdom were so fond of having themselves represented in a writing posture; for that was the occupation to which they owed their rank and power. The road to every office lay open to him who had learnt writing and knew how to express himself in well-chosen terms, and all the other professions were literally under his control.'[1]

Begrich,[2] too, makes the point that the title 'Royal Scribe' appears frequently in Egypt as the honorary title of any high official, including the vizier himself. Yet he tends to look for an intrinsic connection between writing and the office of 'Scribe'. Thus he says that in foreign affairs the 'Scribe' (Schreiber) is the one who carries on diplomatic correspondence and that, since the Pharaohs had a considerable correspondence of this kind, such a function would enhance his importance. Hempel's[3] statement that the simplicity of the Hebrew alphabet as contrasted with Babylonian cuneiform or Egyptian hieroglyphics reduced the dependence of the community on a bureaucracy seems to me to reveal some misunderstanding of the relationship between the mastery of the art of writing and the tenancy of high office. The simpler

[1] A. Erman (tr. A. M. Blackman), *The Literature of the Ancient Egyptians* (1927), pp. xxvii–xxviii. Similarly H. Duesberg, *Les scribes inspirés*, i, pp. 36–37, 193. G. R. Driver, *Semitic Writing From Pictograph to Alphabet* (1948), pp. 71–72. Driver remarks on the wide choice of careers which were open to the man who had mastered the Babylonian cuneiform script. 'For in public esteem "the cuneiform script, the beginning of kingship" as it was called, was regarded as a high road to the highest positions in the state' (p. 72).

[2] J. Begrich, *op. cit.*, pp. 20–23.

[3] J. Hempel, *Die althebräische Literatur und ihr hellenistischjüdisches Nachleben* (1930), p. 55. Similarly W. Zimmerli, *op. cit.*, p. 180.

Hebrew alphabet may have reduced the number of writers or clerks in the service of the state, but it would have no bearing on the composition of the higher reaches of officialdom. This was determined not by the Hebrew system of writing, but by the political structure of the Israelite state and from David on there was a need for such a governing and administrative *élite*, since the community was ruled by the king through such a cadre of officials.

Further light is thrown on the relationship between 'writing' and the title *sōpēr*, as it is used of a leading minister of the king in the Old Testament, by an examination of Akkadian *šapāru* and *šāpirum* (a form cognate to Hebrew *sōpēr*). *Šapāru* means 'to send', 'to entrust with a mission', 'to commission', 'to superintend', 'to communicate', 'to write'. The idea of 'office' or 'managerial responsibility' rather than that of 'writing' is primary. This is borne out by the various meanings of *šāpirum*, 'State Secretary', 'manager', 'agent', 'writer'. Muss-Arnoldt[1] connects the meaning 'to send' for *šapāru* with the third form of Arabic √*sfr* 'to travel' and Arabic *safīr* 'ambassador' should also be noted.

This evidence shows that the meaning 'to write' is on the semantic fringe of *šapāru* and similarly with 'writer' in the case of *šāpirum*.[2] A *šāpirum* is primarily a person who holds a responsible political or administrative office and the meaning 'writer' is developed for the same reasons as those adduced by Erman for the Egyptian title 'Scribe'. The mastery of the complicated system of cuneiform writing was a *sine qua non* for the man who would aspire to responsible office in the state and it would have been impossible to discharge high political or administrative duties, whether executive or advisory, without this mastery of the involved art of written communication.

It is therefore understandable that an association should be established between the holding of office and the art of writing, but this does not give us the right to draw conclusions about the functions of an official or minister who has the title *šāpirum*. Thus there are compounds which define more precisely the offices which

[1] W. Muss-Arnoldt, *A Concise Dictionary of the Assyrian Language* (1905), ii, *s.v. šapāru.* Also Carl Bezold, *Babylonisch-Assyrisches Glossar* (1926). P. Anton Deimal, *Akkadisch-Sumerisches Glossar* (1937), III.2. It is not yet possible to consult the Chicago *Assyrian Dictionary* or the *Akkadisches Handwörterbuch* of W. von Soden for √*špr*.

[2] Cf. H. H. Schaeder, *op. cit.*, p. 39. *Šapāru* has from the primary meaning 'to send a message' developed the meaning 'to write', 'to correspond'.

a *šāpirum* might hold, such as Land Secretary, Secretary of Canal Construction and Secretary of Commerce.[1]

Again there is an Akkadian word (Sumerian loan word) which means precisely 'tablet-writer' (Sumerian DUB SAR, Akkadian *ṭupsarrum*).[2] In such a compound as *ṭupsar* (*sa*) *māti*, 'Land Secretary', *ṭupsar* is the equivalent of *šāpir*.[3] This therefore is another demonstration of the connection between mastery of the art of writing and the rise to high office. The position, then, is that many a *ṭupsarrum* was not a *šāpirum*, but that every *šāpirum* was a *ṭupsarrum*. We have to distinguish between Secretaries of State and run-of-the-mill writers, and we are not to suppose that we can conclude from the title *šāpirum* that the functions of such an official are mainly concerned with writing or correspondence. Gressmann[4] has made this distinction between 'Scribes' *par excellence* who were influential in the highest echelons of government and the ordinary correspondence scribes who were especially needed in the cities of the Orient for the non-alphabetic scripts. Meissner[5] similarly discriminates between 'Secretary' and 'secretary' and notes that the *šāpir* is one of the most frequently mentioned and versatile of officials who might hold such offices as Land Secretary, Secretary of Justice, and Ambassador. We may then conclude this part of the argument with the statement that the idea of 'writing' is associated with the title *šāpirum* only in so far as it was basic to the educational discipline which was an indispensable preparation for positions of power and responsibility in the state.

In the case of Hebrew √*spr*[6] the meanings of the verb are 'counting', 'recounting', 'narrating'. The connection with writing appears only in the participle *sōpēr* which can certainly mean

[1] Carl Bezold, *op. cit., s.v., šāpirum*. B. Meissner, *op. cit.*, i, pp. 122–4. H. H. Schaeder, *op. cit.*, pp. 45–46.

[2] Cf. Carl Bezold, *op. cit., s.v. ṭupsarrum*, contrasts *ṭupsarrum*, 'tablet-writer' with another Sumerian loan word *kuššarum*, 'parchment writer'.

[3] Cf. G. R. Driver, *op. cit.*, p. 62, n. 4. 'That DUB SAR and *šāpir ilki* ("administrator of taxes") are equated in a native syllabary shows how varied the scribe's duties must have been.'

[4] H. Gressmann, *Israels Spruchweisheit im Zusammenhang der Weltliteratur* (1925), p. 47.

[5] B. Meissner, *op. cit.*, i, p. 121. Meissner notes a more limited sense of *šāpirum* in the Assyrian bureaucracy where it is used of a provincial official who is the subordinate of the governor (p. 132).

[6] L. Köhler, *Lexicon in Veteris Testamenti Libros* (1958), *s.v.* √*spr*. Cf. *Ugaritic* √*spr*, G. R. Driver, *Canaanite Myths and Legends* (1956), p. 147.

'writer' and in the noun *sēper* 'book', 'document'. Akkadian *šāpirum* is perhaps our best guide to the elucidation of *sōpēr* as it is used in the Old Testament of a leading minister of the king. Even if the argument be pressed that the Israelite bureaucracy owes much to Egyptian models,[1] the evidence furnished by an exactly analogous form from a cognate language deserves careful consideration. I do not therefore believe that the meaning 'write' can be brought into any closer relationship with the title *sōpēr*, as it is used of a leading official of the king, than that which obtains between 'write' and *šāpirum*.

We are not therefore entitled to assume that *hassōpēr* is the minister who deals with royal, domestic and foreign correspondence and that this is essentially the content of his office. This being so, many of the conjectures which have been made about the content of the office are insecurely founded. Begrich[2] has remarked that the titles *hassōpēr* and *hammazkīr* do not define the functions of these officials and has recorded some of the widely differing conjectures about the roles fulfilled by them. Some of these in respect of the office of *hassōpēr* presuppose an intrinsic connection between it and 'writing', and this is true of Begrich's own suggestion that *hassōpēr* was responsible for managing correspondence—more particularly foreign correspondence.[3]

Moreover, the assumption of Gressmann and others that Shusha[4] and Shebna, two holders of the office of *hassōpēr*, were foreigners is at least partly based on the assumption that there is this intrinsic bond between the office and the art of writing. Gressmann's[5] opinion is that *hassōpēr* was responsible for managing diplomatic correspondence and that at the period when Babylonian cuneiform was the diplomatic language Shusha, a Babylonian, held

[1] See above, p. 23.

[2] J. Begrich, *op. cit.*, pp. 1–2.

[3] See above, p. 24. Also K. Galling, 'Die israelitische Staatsverfassung in ihrer vorderorientalischen Umwelt', p. 40.

[4] M. Noth, *Die Israelitischen Personennamen im Rahmen der gemeinsemitischen Namengebung* (BWANT 3.10, 1928). Seraiah in II Sam. 8.17 is, in Noth's opinion, a textual error (p. 21, n. 1). Its meaning is 'Yahweh is Lord' (or 'Ruler'). √*śrh* is a variant form of √*śrr*; cf. *śar* 'prince', 'ruler' and Akkadian *šarrum* (p. 192, n. 1). L. Köhler, *Lexicon, s.v.*, follows Noth in so far as he understands *miśrā* in Isa. 9.5, 6 [6, 7] to mean 'dominion' and derives it from √*śrh*—a variant form of √*śrr*. In II Sam. 20.25 Noth would write the form as *Šūšā* (p. 258, no. 1328) and similarly in I Kings 4.3 (p. 258, no. 1332) and I Chron. 18.16 (p. 258, no. 1322).

[5] H. Gressmann, *Israels Spruchweisheit*, pp. 49–50. J. Hempel, *op. cit.*, p. 54. A. Bentzen, *Introduction*, i, p. 171.

the office, while in the later period, when Aramaic was the diplomatic language, Shebna, an Aramaean, was its occupant. De Vaux[1] argues that the foreignness of Shusha is shown by the circumstance that he is the only one of David's leading officials whose father's name is not mentioned and that Shebna likewise has no pedigree. The argument with respect to Shusha is, he urges, clinched by the fact that his son Elihoreph has an Egyptian name. De Vaux reads the name as 'Api is my God' and observes that names compounded with Api were a commonplace in Egypt.[2]

It is doubtful whether a case can be made out for the foreignness of these names. Noth[3] understands Shusha (*Šûšā*) as an abbreviated name, only a single consonant (which is duplicated) of the full name being retained. He thinks that we have to do here with pet names which grew out of the nursery and which are so firmly established that the full names on which they are based can no longer be ascertained.[4] *Šeḇnā'* (*Šeḇnā*) is explained by Noth[5] as an abbreviation of *Šᵉḇanyāh(ū)*. *Šbn* is the perfect of a verb whose meaning cannot be ascertained and the name is perhaps a compound of passive participle and genitive, that is, . . . of Yahu. Thus Noth's opinion is that the theophoric element is Yahu (Yahweh) and so the name is *prima facie* Israelite and not foreign.[6]

We come now to Ahikar, who is a counsellor (*y'ṭ*) of all Assyria and seal bearer to Esarhaddon. Ahikar is thus portrayed as the

[1] R. de Vaux, *op. cit.*, pp. 398–400. On Elihoreph, Noth (p. 237, no. 151) says that the meaning of the second element, 'autumn', 'winter', does not seem apt and that the whole cannot be satisfactorily elucidated.

[2] K. Galling, *op. cit.*, pp. 39–40, supposes that Elihoreph and Ahijah were Egyptian and Babylonian respectively and connects this with the fact that diplomatic correspondence had to be carried on in both these languages. With regard to Ahijah the theophoric element *Yah* is *prima facie* evidence that it is an Israelite name.

[3] M. Noth, *op. cit.*, pp. 40–41.

[4] L. Köhler, *Lexicon, s.v. Šawšā'*, cites Aramaic *kyšwš* which he equates with Akkadian *Kī-Šamaš* and suggests that *Šawšā'* is developed from **Šamšā'*. Cf. A. Dupont-Sommer, *RA* 40 (1946), p. 46. Dupont-Sommer notes that *Šamaš* is transliterated *Šawaš* in an Aramaic translation of a Babylonian tablet. Thus in line 1 *Šawaš-uballiṭ* is written for *Šamaš-uballiṭ*; *Bēl-ēṭir-Šamaš* is written *bl'ṭršwš* and *kyšmš* is written *kyšwš*. But the postulated form **Šamšā'* is difficult. Why the emphatic form? This form does not appear in the Aramaic transcriptions cited above.

[5] M. Noth, *op. cit.*, p. 258, nos. 1302, 1303. Cf. W. F. Albright, *BASOR* 79 (1940), p. 28, n. 1. Albright agrees with Noth that *Šeḇnā'* is an abbreviated form, but he suggests that the original is *šûḇ-nā'-Yāhū*, 'Turn, prithee, O Yahweh'.

[6] Isaiah's attack on Shebna in Isa. 22.15ff. and, in particular, his assertion that he had no right to hew out a tomb for himself (22.16) has been thought to point to the foreignness of Shebna (K. Galling, *op. cit.*, p. 40). It will be noticed that in this passage Shebna is described as *ašer 'al habbayiṯ* (cf. II Kings 18.18, where he has the title *hassōp̄ēr*).

king's first minister—his vizier[1]—and this has to be kept in mind[2] in assessing the meaning of *spr ḥkym wmhyr*[3]—another of his titles. In view of this context we should keep the meaning of Akkadian *šāpirum* to the fore when we are translating *spr ḥkym wmhyr*, and in this connection it should be noted that Aramaic *sāpᵉrā'* has been regarded as a loan word from Akkadian and so directly derived from *šāpirum*. Thus Schaeder[4] has argued that Ezra was a Secretary of State in the sense of Akkadian *šāpirum*, and I have pointed to Ezra 4.8–9, 17, 23,[5] where Shimshai who has the title *sāpᵉrā'* is a colleague of leading officials and should therefore be regarded as a high civil servant—again the sense of Akkadian *šāpirum*.

In view of all this I think it is unlikely that *spr ḥkym wmhyr* as used of Ahikar refers to his dexterity or skill as a writer. The translation should rather be 'sagacious and keen-witted statesman' (or 'Secretary of State'). *mhyr* then refers to the agility and sharpness of Ahikar's mind in his role as a practising statesman, and it is these intellectual virtues of political sagacity and mental agility that he seeks to inculcate into Nadin, so that he may be fitted to follow him in high office.[6] *Spr ḥkym wmhyr* occurs in association with such phrases as 'Counsellor (*y'ṭ*) of all Assyria', 'Bearer of the Seal', 'master of good counsel (*'ṭh*) by whose counsel and words all Assyria was (guided)'.[7] Hence the correct interpretation of *spr ḥkym wmhyr* would seem to be 'sagacious and keen-witted Secretary of State' and not 'wise and skilful writer', and the coupling of *ḥkym* with *mhyr* is better suited to the one translation than the other, for it does not seem particularly apposite to couple wisdom with dexterity in writing, but it is apposite to couple sagacity with mental agility as two of the prime virtues of a statesman. The

[1] This is probably a correct assumption, although W. A. Ward, *op. cit.*, pp. 145–6, has pointed out that to be bearer of the royal seal in Egypt was not necessarily to be vizier and that the title was accorded to many other officials of importance besides the vizier.

[2] So H. Gressmann, *Israels Spruchweisheit*, p. 47.

[3] See above, p. 17.

[4] H. H. Schaeder, *op. cit.*, pp. 39ff.: 'The corresponding Aramaic word *sāprā* appears in the older Aramaic as a firm designation of a vocation already in a mark of ownership on a bowl found in Nimrud in Assyria, probably belonging to the 7th century BC. Also on an Assyrian gem which is dated in the 6th century.' Cf. W. Baumgartner, *Lexicon*, *s.v.* *sāpar.

[5] See above, p. 21.

[6] A. E. Cowley, *op. cit.*, p. 212, *Ahikar* i.10, ii.18. Ahikar has taught Nadin wisdom (*ḥkm*) and counsel (*'ṭh*).

[7] A. E. Cowley, *ibid.*, i.3, 4, 7, 12; ii.28; iii.35–36; iv.55, 61.

phrase *spr ḥkym*[1] which is also used of Ahikar points in the same direction, for 'sagacious Secretary of State' is more probable than 'sagacious writer'.

Gressmann[2] has called attention to the use of *māhīr* as a title in Papyrus Anastasi I.[3] This he explains as a Canaanite gloss[4] and an abbreviation of *sōpēr māhīr*. I have some difficulty in following Gressmann's account, but he appears to say that *sōpēr māhīr* is a piece of old Canaanite terminology and that, in its original setting, it means 'dexterous writer'. One must think, says Gressmann, of the cursive script, customary with the Semites as with the Egyptians, of which the scribe was a master. Gressmann, however, agrees with Erman[5] that *māhīr* in Papyrus Anastasi I describes an Egyptian officer who was peripatetic in Syria—'a far-travelled official'. Of this *māhīr* Gressmann says that he was a military officer who was knowledgeable about cartography and geography and who was versed in the languages of the land in which he was operating.

The first question which we have to try to settle is whether *māhīr* in Papyrus Anastasi I is, in fact, a Canaanite gloss and an abbreviation of *sōpēr māhīr* and this is not a simple matter. Brugsch[6] says that Egyptian *mhr* corresponds with Semitic *mhr*, but he does not define the nature of the relationship between the two. Budge[7] does not include *mhr* in his list of non-Egyptian words, whereas Burchardt[8] includes it among his loan words as a very common title of an Egyptian official. Erman and Grapow[9] record it as a fairly common Egyptian word meaning 'slayer', 'young hero', and as the title of a king and a warrior. They appear to accept it as a genuine Egyptian word, although they query whether it may not be a loan word and cite Semitic *mhr*.[10]

[1] A. E. Cowley, *ibid.*, ii.28; iii.35.

[2] H. Gressmann, 'Die neugefundene Lehre des Amenemope und die vorexilische Spruchdichtung Israels', p. 295; *Israels Spruchweisheit*, pp. 49–50.

[3] A. Erman, *op. cit.*, pp. 214–34.

[4] So also J. Hempel, *op. cit.*, p. 54. W. Baumgartner, *Israelitische und altorientalische Weisheit*, p. 20. H. H. Schaeder, *op. cit.*, p. 40. A. Bentzen, *Introduction*, i, p. 170.

[5] A. Erman, *op. cit.*, p. 227, n. 3.

[6] H. Brugsch, *Hieroglyphisch-Demotisches Wörterbuch* (1880), *s.v. mhr*.

[7] E. A. Wallis Budge, *An Egyptian Hieroglyphic Dictionary* (1920), pp. 1305ff.

[8] M. Burchardt, *Die altkanaanäischen Fremdworte und Eigennamen in Ägyptischen* (1909–10), ii, p. 26, no. 486.

[9] A. Erman und H. Grapow, *Das Wörterbuch der ägyptischen Sprache* (1955), ii, pp. 115–16.

[10] I owe the last two references to Professor G. R. Driver, who adds (in a letter)

The phrase 'I am a scribe, a *māhīr*'[1] does seem to indicate that Gressmann's conclusion is correct, particularly since there are other indubitable Semitic glosses in Papyrus Anastasi I. Thus Amenemope is addressed as *sōpēr yōḏē*, 'knowledgeable official'.[2] The sense of *sōpēr māhīr* which best suits this passage is not, however, 'dexterous writer', for Amenemope, as Gressmann knows, is represented as a military official. Hence Erman understands *māhīr* as a Canaanite word for 'nimble', 'adept' and says: 'Amenemope had drawn attention to his deeds and experiences in Syria and proudly assigned himself a foreign designation, that of Mahir, i.e. a hero.'[3] Further the meaning 'warrior' is attested for *mhr* in Ugaritic[4] and so the understanding of *sōpēr māhīr* presupposed by the usage in Papyrus Anastasi I may be 'military official' (a usage of *sōpēr* attested in the Old Testament),[5] since this is the kind of office which Amenemope appears to hold.

The evidence of Papyrus Anastasi I might therefore be thought to point to a meaning of 'military official' for Semitic *sōpēr māhīr*, but it does not support the conclusion that the primary meaning of this Semitic term is 'dexterous writer' as Gressmann supposes.[6] The appearance of the Egyptian word for 'scribe' in the phrase 'I am a scribe, a *māhīr*' does nothing to prove this, since, as we have seen,[7] 'scribe' is a general designation for an Egyptian official and does no more than show that a mastery of the art of writing was an indispensable preliminary for any person aspiring to high office.

I propose now to sum up this part of the argument by calling attention to the contribution made by our discussion of *spr ḥkym wmhyr* in Ahikar to the elucidation of *sōpēr māhīr*. The following are the considerations which are particularly relevant:

---

that Egyptian is partly Semitic and partly Hamitic, that it has many roots and words which also occur in Hebrew and that, as a consequence, it is often difficult to say whether a word has arisen independently, or comes from a proto-Semitic source common to both languages, or is a loan word on one side or the other.

[1] A. Erman, *op. cit.*, p. 227.

[2] A. Erman, *ibid.*, p. 226. H. H. Schaeder, *op. cit.*, p. 40, notes *sōpēr yōḏē* and has no doubt that Gressmann is correct in supposing *māhīr* to be a contraction of *sōpēr māhīr*.

[3] A. Erman, *ibid.*, p. 227.

[4] G. R. Driver, *Canaanite Myths and Legends*, p. 159, *s.v. mhr*. Cf. p. 159, n. 7, where Driver notes *mhr* as an Egyptian word for 'soldier'.

[5] See above, pp. 21-2.

[6] K. Galling, *Die Krise der Aufklärung in Israel* (1952), p. 10, says that the term *sōper māhīr* indicates that dictation was a fundamental part of the scribe's intellectual discipline. This statement assumes the meaning 'dexterous writer'.

[7] See above, pp. 23–24.

(*a*) Ahikar is almost certainly Assyrian in origin. Cowley[1] holds that the Aramaic betrays Persian influence and may be a translation from Persian, but that the original language is, in all probability, Assyrian. He holds that the Ahikar story and proverbs were originally composed in Assyrian *c.* 550 BC and that the date of the Aramaic papyrus is *c.* 430 BC. Sachau[2] connects the Ahikar story with the last decades of the Neo-Babylonian kingdom after the fall of Assyria and thinks that it was probably written between 550 and 450 BC. Ahikar may have been a wise vizier who lived in the days of the Assyrian empire and whose betrayal by his adopted son furnished material for later romances.[3] Causse[4] is wrong in supposing that the Aramaic fragments of Ahikar are in any sense 'Jewish wisdom' and Cowley's remarks on this point are entirely adequate: 'It is not derived from Hebrew sources and there is no reason why we should expect it to be.'[5] If, then, we can conclude that Ahikar originates in Assyria, we are right to be guided by the sense of Akkadian *šāpirum* in making a decision about the meaning of *spr ḥkym wmhyr*.

(*b*) If, as Schaeder[6] supposes, Aramaic *sāpᵉrā'* is a loan word from Akkadian, this establishes even more precisely the semantic relationship between *šāpirum* and *sāpᵉrā'*, and I have noted a passage where the correct translation of *sāpᵉrā'* is 'official' (Ezra 4.8, 9, 17, 23).

(*c*) 'Sagacious and keen-witted Secretary of State' is a translation which better accords with the other functions ascribed to Ahikar than does 'sagacious and dexterous writer'.[7]

[1] A. E. Cowley, *op. cit.*, pp. 205–8.

[2] E. Sachau, *Aramäische Papyrus und Ostraka aus einer jüdischen Militarkolonie zu Elephantiné* (1911), pp. 147–82.

[3] W. Baumgartner, *Israelitische und altorientalische Weisheit*, p. 16, also holds that Ahikar is Assyrian in origin. J. Rendel Harris, in *The Apocrypha and Pseudepigrapha of the Old Testament* (ed. R. H. Charles, 1913), ii, pp. 719–20, holds that the Aramaic papyrus was written between 420 and 400 BC and that the story itself is to be dated between 550 and 450 BC. He supposes that the story was brought from Mesopotamia to Elephantiné, but he believes (*pace* Cowley, *op. cit.*, p. 205) that Aramaic is the original language and that 'we are as near to the first form of an ancient book as we are ever likely to be' (p. 720). He thus excludes the possibility that Ahikar had a prior literary existence in Assyrian and that the Aramaic version is a translation.

[4] A. Causse, *La Sagesse et la propaganda juive à l'époque perse et hellenistique* (BZAW 66, 1936), pp. 148–54.

[5] A. E. Cowley, *op. cit.*, p. 205. Also J. Rendel Harris, *op. cit.*, ii, p. 720: 'There is no sign of a Hebraism anywhere in the book.'

[6] See above, p. 29.

[7] *Pace* H. H. Schaeder, *op. cit.*, p. 50, who explains *spr ḥkym wmhyr* as connected with a supposed pre-Israelite, Canaanite usage of *spr mhyr*, 'dexterous writer'.

(*d*) The Egyptian officer in Papyrus Anastasi I who is called a *māhīr* is portrayed as a 'military officer' or a 'keen-witted officer' rather than as a 'dexterous writer'.

As for the Old Testament evidence, Gressmann[1] calls attention to Prov. 22.29 and to a verse in the Instruction of Amenemope which he identifies as the original of the passage in Proverbs. Amenemope reads:

> As for the scribe who is experienced in his office,
> He will find himself worthy to be a courtier.[2]

And the corresponding lines in Proverbs run:

> You have seen a man who is *māhīr* in his work,
> He will have official standing in the presence of kings.

Gressmann correctly refers both passages to the man who is equipped for high office in the state because of his mental agility and keen grasp of affairs. In view of what I have already said about the title 'Scribe' in Egypt it will be appreciated that the verse from Amenemope does nothing to establish a connection between *māhīr* and skill in writing. Another occurrence of *māhīr* in the Old Testament quite unconnected with writing is Isa. 16.5, where *m^e^hīr ṣeḏeq* means 'swift to dispense justice' or, perhaps, 'expert[3] in dispensing justice'.[4]

On the other hand, there is no doubt that *sōpēr* has the meaning 'writer' in biblical Hebrew, for Baruch (Jer. 36.32) is such a writer or amanuensis. Also Ezek. 9.2, 3 mentions a man clothed in linen with the *qeseṯ* ('palette' or 'writing-case') of a *sōpēr* on his loins. This is a reference to a secretary with a small *s* and the same is true of the writers in Esth. 3.12 and 8.9, who draft edicts at the Persian

[1] H. Gressmann, 'Die neugefundene Lehre des Amenemope', p. 295.

[2] F. Ll. Griffith, 'The Teaching of Amenophis, the son of Kanakht. Papyrus B.M. 10474', *JEA* 12 (1926), p. 224. John Wilson in *Ancient Near Eastern Texts Relating to the Old Testament* (ed. J. B. Pritchard, 1955), p. 424 (xxvii.16–17).

[3] So E. Ullendorff, 'Contribution of South Semitics to Hebrew', *VT* 6 (1956), p. 195. Ullendorff notes that *mhr* in Ethiopic means 'to teach' and in the reflexive stem 'to learn'. He suggests that the basic meaning of this Semitic word is 'to be skilled' which embraces the idea of 'speed' (Hebrew) as well as that of 'knowledge' (Ethiopic). He further argues that the adjective *māhīr* in biblical Hebrew means 'practised', 'expert', 'skilled' rather than 'quick', 'speedy'.

[4] Cf. H. L. Ginsberg, 'Some Emendations in Isaiah', *JBL* 69 (1950), pp. 51–60. I am not convinced by Ginsberg's reasons for emending *m^e^hīr ṣeḏeq* (pp. 54–55). In particular I do not understand why he says that the *scriptio defectiva* is wholly anomalous. Apart from this he observes that elsewhere in biblical Hebrew *māhīr* occurs only as an epithet of *sōpēr* and is not used in the construct state except in this passage. These are not sufficient reasons for questioning the reading *m^e^hīr ṣeḏeq*.

court (*sōpᵉrē hammelek*). Shemaiah, who is called *hassōpēr* in I Chron. 24.6, is also a writer whose job is to record the rota for priestly duties which has been devised. This he does in the presence of the king, his chief political advisers (*haśśārīm*), the two chief priests and other senior priests and levites.

Zadok (*hassōpēr*), who is mentioned in Neh. 13.13, has the important administrative assignment of supervising the tithe of grain, wine and oil which is brought into the storehouses and this is a responsibility which he shares with a priest and a levite. These usages therefore illustrate something of the gradations in meaning of *sōpēr* from 'writer' through 'administrator' (in various grades) to 'Secretary of State'.[1]

Further *sōpēr māhīr* can have the meaning 'dexterous writer' in biblical Hebrew, as is certainly the case in Ps. 45.2 [1]: 'My tongue is the pen of a dexterous writer.' This, in its context, is a metaphor which calls attention to the fluency of the psalmist's speech and so *māhīr* must be referred to the dexterity of the writer—to his smooth-flowing hand. This may also be true of Ezra 7.6, where Ezra is said to be a *sōpēr māhīr*[2] in the *tōrā* of Moses which Yahweh, the God of Israel, had given. This, however, should probably be regarded as a Jewish paraphrase of Ezra's official Aramaic title, which is 'Secretary of the Law of the God of Heaven' (Ezra 7.12, 21), and I believe that Schaeder[3] is right in regarding this as a Persian Secretariat, so that Ezra is a 'Secretary' in the sense of Akkadian *šāpirum*.

Schaeder[4] holds that Ezra 7.6 is an abbreviation by the Chronicler of the full title which appears in 7.12, 21. He urges that the Chronicler did not understand the technical sense of the title and that he gave his own exposition of it in 7.11b, 'scribe of the words of the commandments of Yahweh and his statutes concerning Israel'.[5] According to Schaeder the Chronicler's understanding of

[1] H. H. Schaeder, *op. cit.*, pp. 45–46, observes that in the ancient East 'scribe' had from a very early time a wide range of meaning. Cf. B. Meissner, *op. cit.*, i, p. 121. Also S. N. Kramer, *History Begins At Sumer*[2] (1961), pp. 35–36. Of the position of scribes in ancient Sumer, Kramer says: 'There were junior and "high" scribes, royal and temple scribes, scribes who were highly specialized for particular categories of administrative activities and scribes who became leading officials in the government.'

[2] Cf. E. Ullendorff, *op. cit.*, p. 195, who urges that *māhīr* points to Ezra's knowledge or skill rather than his speed as a writer.

[3] H. H. Schaeder, *op. cit.*, pp. 43ff. A. Bentzen, *Introduction*, i, p. 170.

[4] H. H. Schaeder, *ibid.*, pp. 50–51.

[5] *sōpēr dibᵉrē miṣwōt YHWH wᵉḥuqqāw ʿal-Yiśrāʾēl.*

Ezra maintains some connection with the Persian title, but the special nuance of the latter has faded and Ezra is no longer important as a Persian official but as one who restored the Jewish community. Ezra is now the 'scribe' who brought the Law of Moses, the connoisseur of the Law, the scholar. This would mean that *sōpēr māhīr* in Ezra 7.6 hovers between 'keen-witted Secretary of State' and 'dexterous writer' or 'skilful scholar'.

Schaeder also argues that in naming Ezra *sōpēr māhīr* the Chronicler is taking over a term which had currency in Canaan in the pre-Israelite period and is found in Ahikar. I have already given reasons for my dissent from this part of his argument.[1] I agree, however, with his statement that *sōpēr māhīr* as interpreted by the Chronicler is close to late Jewish usage, since the writer's dexterity is represented as employed with the Law. Thus the meaning 'dexterous writer' or 'skilful scholar' in Ezra 7.6 is connected with the Jewish reorientation of the office of *sōpēr* in which Ezra would appear to have played an influential role. This relates to the post-exilic development of the office of *sōpēr* in the Jewish community and is a complicated problem with which I do not propose to deal in this present work. It will be sufficient to say that there is an ambivalence in the title *sōpēr* as applied to Ezra.[2] If he is a Persian Secretary, he is also the representative of the legalistic piety of Babylonian Jewry, and the object of his mission is to promote the enforcement of a normative and written *tōrā* of Moses within the Jerusalem community. He aims at making them the people of the Law to the extent that their corporate life will be exhaustively regulated by it, and so the meaning 'dexterous writer' or 'skilful scholar' has a special appropriateness in connection with the claims of this written Law.

Hence in explaining *sōpēr māhīr*, 'dexterous writer' or 'skilful scholar' there are three considerations which should be adduced:

[1] See above, pp. 28ff. Also H. H. Schaeder, *ibid.*, pp. 39, 41, where he argues that *sōpēr* as used of Ezra by the Chronicler is not to be derived from *Hebrew* √*spr*, 'to count', but is an assimilation of Akkadian *šāpirum* to Canaanite *sōpēr* (p. 39). This statement implies, as his further remarks (pp. 40, 50) show, that the postulated Canaanite *sōpēr māhīr* means 'dexterous writer' and this is the conclusion which I have challenged.

[2] Cf. H. H. Schaeder, *ibid.*, pp. 39, 42, who says that Ezra was both *Schreiber* and *Schriftgelehrter*. 'His role is a double one. He stands as Secretary in the Persian kingdom and as scholar among his people' (p. 39). Also: 'The shift of meaning from "Secretary" to "scholar" is thus immediately connected with the designation of Ezra, and the Chronicler is the first witness for this new usage' (p. 42).

(*a*) The meaning 'write' is secondary in the case of Akkadian *šapāru, šāpirum* and the meanings of the verb in Hebrew √*spr* also point to the secondary character of the meaning 'write'.

(*b*) The acceptance of the normative, written Law by the post-exilic Jewish community influenced the meaning of *sōpēr*.

(*c*) *Māhīr* in *sōpēr māhīr* is accommodated to the changed sense of *sōpēr* certainly in Ps. 45.2 [1]. *Sōpēr māhīr* in Ahikar means 'keen-witted Secretary of State' and in Ps. 45.2 it means 'dexterous writer'.

We can now consider whether this discussion can be taken any further by giving attention to the schools which produced this educated class of men of whom we have been speaking. It is a fact that these schools were attached to temples,[1] but the misinterpretation of this has given rise to certain misconceptions. It is, for example, not obvious to me that the existence of temple schools is in itself an indication that the literature used for the instruction of the apprentice sage was cultic and so a pointer to the cultic character of the wisdom literature.[2] Erman[3] comments on the kind of literature copied out by the boys at the school built by Rameses II on the west bank of Thebes and observes that there are certain books which turn up again and again among the excavated material. These are the *Instruction of King Amenemhet*, the *Instruction of Duauf* and the *Hymn to the Nile*. He notices that the same three compositions occur together in two school papyri (Papyrus Sallier II and Papyrus Anastasi VII) whose provenance was

[1] On the temple schools built by Rameses II see A. Erman, *op. cit.*, p. 185. L. Dürr, 'Das Erziehungswesen im Alten Testament und im Antiken Orient', *Mitteilungen der vorderasiatisch Gesellschaft*, 36 (1932), pp. 17–19. On the Sumerian school see S. N. Kramer, 'Sumerian Literary Texts from Nippur in the Museum of the Ancient Orient at Istanbul', *AASOR* 23 (1943–4), pp. 36–38; *History Begins At Sumer*, pp. 36–41. On temple schools in Babylonia see H. Duesberg, *op. cit.*, i, p. 38. B. Meissner, *op. cit.*, ii, pp. 325–30. On the temple school associated with the temple of Baal at Ugarit see C. F. A. Schaeffer, *The Cuneiform Texts of Ras Shamra- Ugarit* (1939), pp. 34–35. R. de Langhe, *Les textes Ras Shamra- Ugarit et leurs rapports avec le milieu biblique de l'Ancien Testament* (1945), i, pp. 333–5. S. Mowinckel, 'Psalms and Wisdom' (Rowley Festschrift), p. 207, supposes that there was a school for scribes associated with the Jerusalem temple. Also H. L. Jansen, *op. cit.*, p. 57. W. Baumgartner, *Israelitische und altorientalische Weisheit*, p. 21, cites as evidence for the existence of special schools for scribes in Palestine the name *Qiryaṭ-sōpēr*, 'scribe city' or *Qiryaṭ-sēper*, 'book city'.

[2] A. Bentzen, *Introduction*, i, pp. 174–5, disagrees with the conclusion of I. Engnell (*Gamla Testamentet* I, pp. 57, 62, 64) that wisdom literature has its origin in cultic literature, but he, nevertheless, says that the existence of temple schools is 'a strong circumstance in favour of the assumption' (p. 175).

[3] A. Erman, *op. cit.*, pp. 185–6.

apparently Memphis and which were evidently basic texts in the school curriculum. This evidence lends no support to Jansen's supposition that the texts used in the schools of the ancient East were an amalgam of this-worldly wisdom and cultic literature. Jansen argues that in these temple schools both the wisdom books composed by this or that vizier and the liturgical literature of the temple were in regular use and that 'in this milieu was consummated the blend of worldly wisdom and religio-ethical reflections'.[1] Not even the *Hymn to the Nile* could, in Erman's opinion, be described as cultic literature, for of it he says[2] that, although the Nile was regarded as a god, it did not, unlike the other great divinities, have a regular organized cult, so that the hymn is different in character from other hymns to deities and is not representative of cultic literature.

The evidence from Sumer points in the same direction, as will be seen from the following statement of Kramer:

> As for the literary and creative aspects of the Sumerian curriculum, it consisted primarily in studying, copying and imitating the large and diversified group of literary compositions which must have originated and developed mainly in the latter half of the third millennium BC. These ancient works, running into the hundreds, were almost all poetic in form, ranging in length from less than fifty lines to close to a thousand. Those recovered to date are chiefly of the following genres: myths and epic tales in the form of narrative poems celebrating the deeds and exploits of the Sumerian gods and heroes; hymns to gods and kings; lamentations bewailing the destruction of Sumerian cities; wisdom compositions including proverbs, fables and essays.[3]

There is surely some confusion in the supposition that temple schools in themselves point to the cultic character of wisdom literature. It is to be expected that the temple would be the nurse of education in the ancient Near East as the Church was in the West in the Middle Ages, but the schools founded by cathedrals were grammar schools and not seminaries. There is no reason to suspect that the temple schools of the ancient Near East were less devoted to the basic elements of academic discipline or that there was necessarily a cultic bias in the forms of literature employed.

[1] H. L. Jansen, *op. cit.*, p. 57.
[2] A. Erman, *ibid.*, p. 146.
[3] S. N. Kramer, *History Begins At Sumer*, p. 39.

Although Östborn's[1] statement that both priests and wise men were part of the establishment is correct, he is excessively influenced by two passages (Jer. 2.8; 8.8), which stand somewhat apart from the other passages in Isaiah and Jeremiah in which the *ḥᵃkāmīm* are mentioned, in drawing his conclusions about the nature of the office.[2] He then says that owing to the close ties between the priests and the sages it is not an easy task to distinguish between priestly (cultic) literature and wisdom literature. It is true that some of the *ḥᵃkāmīm* would find their way into the service of the temple either as administrators or as scholars devoted to sacred learning or as wisdom teachers at a temple school where they would be physically adjacent to cultic officials, but if we are to have a balanced account of the matter, it will have to be kept in mind that the *ḥᵃkāmīm* had generally closer connections with the civil or political establishment than with the religious.[3]

Moreover, as Östborn[4] himself recognizes, the piety which mingles with the wisdom literature is not so much cultic piety as legal piety. This is a distinction which has to be maintained, even if Östborn's assumption that the wisdom teachers took over legal instruction from the priests and that the ultimate predominance of Law in wisdom literature was a sequel to its predominance in priestly instruction were thought to be correct.

It has been remarked that these schools were not the agency of universal education but were the preserve of the children of the *élite*. On the temple school built by Rameses II Dürr[5] observes that it belonged to the amenities of the court and that to attend it was to go into residence, and Jansen[6] notes that the pupils for the temple schools in Egypt came from the top layer of society, being the children of courtiers, royal officials and temple personnel. The situation was similar in Babylonia[7] and Kramer[8] has said of the Sumerian school that the fathers of the pupils 'were the wealthier citizens of the urban communities'.

[1] G. Östborn, *op. cit.*, p. 113.
[2] See below, pp. 102ff.
[3] See below, pp. 65ff.
[4] G. Östborn, *op. cit.*, p. 126.
[5] L. Dürr, *op. cit.*, p. 17.
[6] H. L. Jansen, *op. cit.*, p. 57.
[7] L. Dürr, *op. cit.*, pp. 68–69.
[8] S. N. Kramer, *History Begins At Sumer*, p. 37.

Such schools would educate priests for the temple and scholars for sacred learning, but they provided recruits for the learned professions in general and notably for the higher offices of state. Duesberg[1] discusses the choice of careers open to the 'scribe' and says that there were many portfolios in the administration as well as openings in the temple from which he could choose. He is, however, aware that, although both sages and priests belonged to the establishment, their respective spheres of influence tended to be separate and distinct. Dürr[2] says of the Egyptian schools that they were devoted to the training of one class, the 'scribes', and that such wisdom as the school offered was highly valued as opening the door to the highest offices in the state. Of the Sumerian school Kramer[3] says that its function was to train 'scribes' to satisfy the administrative and economic demands of the country, primarily those of the temple and the palace, and that this continued to be its principal function throughout its existence.

Driver[4] notes the existence of two types of schools in Babylonia; there was 'the tablet-house' (*bīt ṭuppate*) which was a school where reading and writing were taught, and another institution, 'the house of wisdom' (*bīt mumme*) where higher education was given.[5] Driver continues: 'There, presumably, the youthful aspirants for a learned career, seated on benches of stone without backs, studied mathematics and astronomy, medicine, magic arts and theology and all the varied branches of "the learning and tongue of the Chaldaeans" (Dan. 1.4).'[6]

We are, then, to envisage a school where the fundamental disciplines of reading and writing were mastered and a more advanced institution where the various subjects of a more specialized higher education were pursued. We have to remember, however, that the study of writing itself was not merely an elementary discipline and that a knowledge of Sumerian as well as of the native Akkadian was required if the aspirant was to be not just a 'school writer' (*ṭupsar mumme*) but a 'master of language' (*bēl lišāni*).[7] It is

[1] H. Duesberg, *op. cit.*, i, p. 37. Similarly L. Dürr, *op. cit.*, pp. 68–69.
[2] L. Dürr, *ibid.*, p. 19.
[3] S. N. Kramer, *op. cit.*, p. 36.
[4] G. R. Driver, *Semitic Writing*, pp. 64–65.
[5] Cf. B. Meissner, *op. cit.*, ii, pp. 325–30. L. Dürr, *op. cit.*, pp. 68–69.
[6] G. R. Driver, *ibid.*, p. 65.
[7] G. R. Driver, *ibid.*, p. 66, n. 3 and 4. Cf. L. Dürr, *ibid.*, p. 69: 'The main part and foundation of higher education was the art of the scribe.' Cf. A. Erman, *op. cit.*, p. 186.

possible, then, to distinguish between 'writer' (*ṭupsarrum*) and 'sage' (*emqum*) and to correlate this distinction with the lower and higher schools of learning, and Driver has noted that the man who enters 'the house of wisdom' is called *emqum*.[1]

All this perhaps throws some light on the problem of the relationship between *sōpēr* and *ḥāḵām* in the setting of the Old Testament.[2] Many a *ṭupsarrum* was not an *emqum*, for one could have the qualifications of a writer or clerk, but not the higher education which was the gateway to positions of power and responsibility in the community. Something of the nature of this higher education in Babylonia is indicated by the account in Dan. 1.4. The Jewish youths who were chosen to train for the Babylonian higher civil service had to attain exacting physical and intellectual standards. It was necessary that they should have a good presence and an aptitude for all wisdom (*maśkīlīm b*^{e}*ḵol ḥoḵmā*). In addition to having this insight into learning (*m*^{e}*ḇīnē maddāʿ*) they required the strength (*kōaḥ*) to stand in the palace of the king. This passage illustrates well the close connections of old wisdom with the educational discipline prescribed for those who would aspire to positions of responsibility in the state.

We may, then, make this point by saying that every *šāpirum* was an *emqum*, for it was an intellectual *élite*, prepared by a prolonged and severe intellectual discipline, who were selected for high political and administrative offices. Thus Ahikar who is a Secretary of State (*spr*) and a counsellor (*yʿṭ*) is also wise (*ḥkym*) and is described as a 'wise and keen-witted Secretary of State' or a 'wise Secretary of State'.[3] It is true that we have to reckon with the ambivalence of *sōpēr* in Hebrew, but those who occupied eminent positions in the government of Judah, whether they are called *sōp*^{e}*rīm* or *yōʿ*^{a}*ṣīm* or *śārīm*, are certainly *ḥ*^{a}*ḵāmīm*[4] and, in particular,

[1] G. R. Driver, *ibid.*, p. 65, n. 5. W. von Soden, *Akkadisches Handwörterbuch*, Lieferung 3 (1960), *s.v.*, *emqum* or *enqum* = *Hebrew ʿmq*, 'deep', 'profound'.

[2] J. Lindblom, 'Wisdom in the Old Testament Prophets' (Rowley Festschrift), p. 195, attempts to elucidate this relationship on the basis of two passages (Jer. 2.8; 8.8) where the meaning of *ḥāḵām* deviates from what is normal in the other places where it is used by Isaiah and Jeremiah (see above, p. 38, and below, pp. 65ff.). Lindblom says that the *sōpēr* in these two passages is the one who drafts the laws, while it is the business of the *ḥāḵām* to expound them. Cf. H. L. Jansen, *op. cit.*, p. 58, who explains Jer. 8.8 on the assumption that the *sōp*^{e}*rīm* mentioned in this passage began as copyists, but then aspired to be exegetes also (see below, pp. 102ff.).

[3] See above, p. 17.

[4] Cf. H. L. Jansen, *op. cit.*, pp. 59–60, who urges that a rigid distinction between *sōpēr* and *ḥāḵām* cannot be maintained in the age of Ben Sira, when the two titles are

it is clear that the *ḥᵃkāmîm* against whom the polemic of Isaiah and Jeremiah is directed are, for the most part,[1] eminent statesmen.

This being so, I am puzzled by Scott's[2] statement that the *ḥᵃkāmîm* are a class or profession who do not appear until the time of Hezekiah. The question of the earlier existence of such a class in Judah is not bound up, as Scott supposes, with the other question whether or not Solomon was the author of any part of the Israelite wisdom literature. Pfeiffer[3] also says that professional wise men are mentioned in Judah for the first time in the period of Isaiah and what he implies by this, I think, is that such a class did not exist prior to this period. His statement is made in the context of a discussion of the dating of the various collections in the book of Proverbs and it is plain from this that Pfeiffer, like Scott, envisages these *ḥᵃkāmîm* primarily as editors and compilers of the wisdom literature. So also with Baumgartner's[4] remark that the hitherto oral transmission of the wisdom literature may have given place to writing by Hezekiah's time. The intention of this statement is to connect the *ḥᵃkāmîm* of whom we hear from Isaiah and Jeremiah with the writing down of the wisdom literature and so to explain their emergence at this period.

Scott[5] further observes that it is not certain whether *ḥākām* in particular circumstances is a descriptive epithet or is the designation of a recognized group, even a profession. He appears to make a distinction between *ḥᵃkāmîm* and *sōpᵉrîm* and of the latter he says: 'On the other hand the scribes, attached to the court and the temple, and their colleagues whose services were made more generally available were professional. Men like Hushai and Ahithophel who were members of the king's privy council and teachers who assembled and taught the materials of wisdom are to be classed in the same way.'[6]

---

interchangeable, and that this equation may go back to the time of Jeremiah. Jansen, however, thinks of these men as authors or collectors of the wisdom literature and neglects their political role.

[1] See below, pp. 102ff.

[2] R. B. Y. Scott, 'Solomon and the Beginnings of Wisdom in Israel' (Rowley Festschrift), pp. 272–4.

[3] R. H. Pfeiffer, *Introduction*, p. 659.

[4] W. Baumgartner, 'The Wisdom Literature' (*The Old Testament and Modern Study*), p. 214. Cf. A. Bentzen, *Introduction*, i, pp. 169–70.

[5] R. B. Y. Scott, 'Priesthood, Prophecy, Wisdom and the Knowledge of God', *JBL* 80 (1961), p. 10.

[6] *Loc. cit.*

I am not at all sure how this statement is to be understood. Scott may be saying that Hushai and Ahithophel were *sōpᵉrīm* and not *ḥᵃḵāmīm*, although it seems to be more likely that what he intends to say is that they were both *sōpᵉrīm* and *ḥᵃḵāmīm*. The intention of his general statement would then be that not all *ḥᵃḵāmīm* are *sōpᵉrīm*, that is, *ḥāḵām* is not everywhere the title of a higher civil servant. If this is what he is saying, I have no occasion for disagreeing with him. The only question which is at stake in the context of the present discussion is whether the *ḥᵃḵāmīm* attacked by Isaiah and Jeremiah were key political advisers and executives. Scott[1] agrees that Jer. 18.18 may refer to the political advice given by royal counsellors, but he then goes on to say: 'On the other hand the wise man is here correlated with two religious authorities and the wise whom Jeremiah actually attacks are the scribes who handle the "Law of the Lord", presumably the Deuteronomic covenant law book.' This is contrary to the facts and can apply only to two passages (Jer. 2.8; 8.8–9) which stand apart from the main group.[2] Gressmann[3] acutely comments on the grounds of disagreement between prophet and *ḥāḵām* and notes that the *ʿēṣā* of *ḥāḵām* and *zāqēn* was practical, empirical wisdom.[4] He observes correctly that such *ḥᵃḵāmīm* or *sōpᵉrīm* occupied the highest positions of state in Judah in the pre-exilic period.

Scott's assumption would seem to be that the *ḥᵃḵāmīm* who are attacked by Isaiah and Jeremiah are purely and simply men of letters. On the contrary these *ḥᵃḵāmīm* are to be equated with a class of officials who existed from the time of David onwards, and the emergence of such a governing and administrative class has been correctly correlated with the fundamental political reorganization of Israel which was carried through by David and Solomon. Israel became a state with a new political structure which demanded the creation of a cadre of royal officials through whom the king governed his people. There is abundant evidence for this and it is generally accepted. Thus Duesberg[5] says that from the

[1] *Ibid.*, p. 3.

[2] See Part Two.

[3] H. Gressmann, 'Die neugefundene Lehre des Amenemope', pp. 289ff. So also J. Lindblom, 'Wisdom in the Old Testament', pp. 192–4, who says that Isaiah and Jeremiah recognized the *ḥᵃḵāmīm* as a class in the circles of the government.

[4] See below, pp. 55ff.

[5] H. Duesberg, *op. cit.*, i, pp. 144–8, 193, 209. J. Begrich, 'Sōfēr und Mazkīr', pp. 10–11, remarks that in Saul's kingdom there was no room for government

time of Solomon the Israelite state was modelled on the great states of the ancient Near East and so acquired a structure similar to that of Egypt. He points to Solomon's trade relations with Hiram and his alliance with Egypt through marriage and he notices that the creation of the new state was not the work of the king alone, but that with the king in this new political structure there was associated a class of royal officials who had to do with the army, finance, foreign embassies and administration. Such officials were a 'people of the king' and had a common interest with him in maintaining the régime and suppressing popular resistance and discontent.

This discussion does, however, raise the question of the identity of the practitioners of the wisdom literature and, in this connection, Gressmann[1] observes that the 'scribe', although not primarily a man of letters, had to master foreign languages for the purposes of diplomacy, and that in so doing he acquired a knowledge of foreign literatures and assisted in their dissemination. He continues: 'The Egyptian scribe who, as the Amarna letters testify, learned the Babylonian language by means of the Adapa myth in order to equip himself for diplomatic correspondence would thereby become knowledgeable in Babylonian literature and a disseminator of it.'[2] And again: 'We know who the bearers of this international literature were. They designated themselves "the wise", that is, the cultured or educated. According to their profession they were, for the most part, "scribes"—not ordinary correspondence scribes who were especially needed in the cities of the Orient for the non-alphabetic scripts, but scribes *par excellence* who in the service of the State, administration or army were influential in the highest circles of ministers and officials.'[3]

Similarly Baumgartner[4] says that in both Egypt and Babylonia wisdom is located in the circle of a high scribal establishment which plays an important role in the political and cultural life of the time and that these 'scribes' have to be distinguished from

---

officials; the need for them first arose as a consequence of political reorganization under David and the probability is that they were created on the model of similar offices outside Israel. Cf. K. Galling, *Die Krise der Aufklärung in Israel* (1952), pp. 5ff.

[1] H. Gressmann, 'Die neugefundene Lehre des Amenemope', p. 295.
[2] H. Gressmann, *ibid.*, p. 295.
[3] H. Gressmann, *Israels Spruchweisheit*, p. 47.
[4] W. Baumgartner, *Israelitische und altorientalische Weisheit*, pp. 19–20.

mere writers. This seems to me to put the matter in the right perspective and it may not be going too far to say, as Gressmann does, that these men, although primarily statesmen and administrators, were 'born middlemen in the international exchange of literature'.[1]

We should then envisage a somewhat similar situation in pre-exilic Judah and should not underestimate the political role of the *ḥᵃḵāmîm*. Neither Eissfeldt[2] nor Mowinckel[3] seems to me altogether to do justice to their political importance. Eissfeldt says that their activity was not of a purely literary and academic kind and that in addition to their literary and editorial activities they had teaching duties. Mowinckel tends to think of them only as learned writers who were closely connected with temple singers and poets. Bentzen[4] says that during Solomon's reign Israel was opened up to the surrounding world in a way which gave the circles cultivating the wisdom literature importance for the public life of Israel. This is obscure, but I take it to mean that the introduction of the wisdom literature to Israel is to be correlated with the structure of Solomon's state and the creation of a new class of officials—the *sōpᵉrîm* or *ḥᵃḵāmîm*. This would agree with Humbert's[5] understanding of the matter. He argues that the wisdom literature first appeared in Israel in Solomon's reign and that its appearance is to be connected with Solomon's new establishment or bureaucracy.

The wisdom literature is, for the most part, a product not of full-time men of letters and academics,[6] but of men of affairs in high places of state, and the literature in some of its forms bears the marks of its close association with those who exercise the skills of statecraft. This is particularly evident in the case of the Egyptian 'Instruction'[7] whose aim is to lay down the first principles of states-

[1] H. Gressmann, 'Die neugefundene Lehre des Amenemope', p. 295. Cf. *Israels Spruchweisheit*, p. 50.

[2] O. Eissfeldt, *Introduction to the Old Testament* (tr. P. R. Ackroyd, 1965), p. 86.

[3] S. Mowinckel, 'Psalms and Wisdom' (Rowley Festschrift), p. 207.

[4] A. Bentzen, *Introduction*, i, p. 169.

[5] P. Humbert, *Recherches sur les sources égyptiennes de la littérature sapientiale d'Israel* (1929), p. 181. Similarly B. Gemser, *Sprüche Salomos* (HAT), p. 2, who says that in the reign of Solomon the Israelite state was organized on the model of the great and small oriental kingdoms and that wisdom was fostered in connection with this bureaucracy.

[6] It is not my intention to assert that there were no *ḥᵃḵāmîm* fully employed in scholarship or letters or as wisdom teachers. Cf. S. N. Kramer, *History Begins At Sumer*, pp. 36–37. Kramer says that an academic tradition grew up in connection with the Sumerian school, but that its main aim throughout its existence was to supply 'scribes' for state and temple. See below, pp. 102ff.

[7] *Ancient Near Eastern Texts* (ed. J. B. Pritchard), pp. 412ff.

manship and to define the fundamental intellectual attitudes which are desiderated for the aspiring statesman or administrator. The association of this *genre* with the practice of government is underlined by the circumstance that the authors of these pieces are sometimes represented as having spent a lifetime in the service of the state in the highest offices. Humbert[1] notes that the most ancient examples of the Egyptian 'Instruction' were composed by kings and viziers and were addressed to their sons in order to prepare them for succession to office, and Gressmann[2] observes that this literature is clearly connected with the vocation of 'scribe' and the tasks of government.

Indeed, the second and higher stage of education in Egypt was not completed in school but in a government department where the student had a more senior official as his tutor. From this it is clear that he was serving his apprenticeship as a bureaucrat and was being groomed for competence and grasp in administration and government.[3] This practical aspect of the higher educational process in Egypt is illustrated by Erman's observation that officials of the most varied kinds were occupied with the education of these apprentices.[4] The Egyptian 'Instruction' is the instrument of a specialized higher education and, besides dealing with *mores* and protocol, its purpose is to cultivate in the apprentice official an intellectual probity and fastidiousness and a maturity of judgment which will enable him to cope with complicated political and administrative problems.[5] There is a sense in which this instruction is authoritative in so far as its aim is to make available a bank of practical wisdom accumulated from the experience of those who have in the past shown themselves to be the most shrewd and perceptive men of affairs.[6] It is not authoritative, however, in the sense of recommending a doctrinaire approach to politics or in prescribing a simple set of rules. The 'Instruction' therefore contains more than vocational training; it supplies education with an

[1] P. Humbert, *op. cit.*, pp. 61–62.

[2] H. Gressmann, *Israels Spruchweisheit*, pp. 48–49. Also T. E. Peet, *A Comparative Study of the Literatures of Egypt, Palestine and Mesopotamia* (1931), pp. 100–1. J. Fichtner, *op. cit.*, pp. 13ff. W. Zimmerli, *op. cit.*, p. 180. H. Duesberg, *op. cit.*, i, p. 448. A. Erman, *op. cit.*, p. xxviii.

[3] Cf. A. Erman, *ibid.*, p. 186. L. Dürr, *op. cit.*, p. 17.

[4] A. Erman, *ibid.*, p. 188.

[5] Cf. L. Dürr, *op. cit.*, pp. 5–6.

[6] Cf. J. Fichtner, *op. cit.*, pp. 13ff.

emphatic practical orientation, but yet it is education, because it enshrines certain educational ideals and values.

There is consequently a particular mental climate which is congenial to these *sōpᵉrīm* or *ḥᵃḵāmīm*; there are well-defined intellectual attitudes which they cherish in connection with the maintenance of high professional standards. This posture might be summed up as 'humanism' only I should have to say immediately that I should be using 'humanism' in a more restricted sense than is usually conveyed by those who speak of the humanism of the age of Solomon or who refer to this period as one of 'enlightment'.[1] By the humanism of these statesmen I mean their confidence that an intellectual *élite* properly disciplined by an arduous process of education can attain to such a mental grasp and delicacy of judgment as to be consistently clear thinkers, perceptive policy-makers and incisive men of action, poised between the extremes of impetuosity and indecision. Gressmann[2] has something like this in mind when he speaks of wisdom as practical worldly shrewdness and acquaintance with gentlemanly procedures in intercourse, not only in the outward sense of polish, tact and good manners, but also inwardly as a noble cast of thought and distinguished pattern of action.

'Humanism' in this context is not a total philosophy of life but principally an intellectual posture with which to confront the complex business of statesmanship. It may also refer to the refined cultural and literary tastes of this educated class, but it is its application to their approach to statecraft that I have mainly in mind. In this area of professional interest and responsibility they believe that an open, uncommitted approach which emphasizes strict intellectual probity and refuses to take one step beyond the evidence is the best way of conducting the business of a state. The sins which they abhor in this context are those which result from slack or shoddy thinking and they are severe on the man who is indiscreet or rash or garrulous in his speech. They admire the person who says little but thinks hard and who applies a sharp and disciplined mind to every facet of a situation before he commits himself to an opinion or a policy. Their ideals are thus intellectual

[1] See below, pp. 48ff.

[2] H. Gressmann, *Israels Spruchweisheit*, pp. 50–51. Cf. E. Sellin, *Introduction to the Old Testament* (tr. W. Montgomery, 1923), pp. 206–7. Cf. W. Zimmerli, *op. cit.*, pp. 178–9.

honesty, rigour and probity and they are convinced that it is such a disciplined empiricism which qualifies a man to administer and govern a state.

This intellectual reserve of the Israelite *sōpᵉrim* or *ḥᵃḵāmîm* and the absence of ethical commitment which we have noticed in the vocabulary of old wisdom do not indicate that these men were necessarily hostile or indifferent to religious belief and morality, but only that they were persuaded that the world in which they had to operate and take decisions was not amenable to the assumptions of religious belief or to a black and white ethical terminology.[1] In saying this I am not altogether at one with von Rad.[2] He speaks acutely of the undoctrinaire, flexible and factual character of this wisdom. It engages itself without illusion with what is given; it is preoccupied with what is possible and has something of an outspoken realism, even opportunism. My difficulty with von Rad's analysis is his assumption that the *ḥᵃḵāmîm* set such limits to the operation of *'ēṣā* as to preclude the possibility of a conflict between its claims and those of the *dāḇār* of Yahweh. The possibility of conflict between the political judgment of these men and the claims of a revealed and authoritative word of Yahweh was only too real and, when the authority of Yahweh's *dāḇār* was invoked in connection with complex and crucial political policies, the conflict was actualized.[3] The *ḥᵃḵāmîm* were satisfied that they would have failed in the discharge of their public responsibility had they allowed doctrinaire assumptions—even assumptions which derived from faith in Yahweh—to influence their judgment. In their professional capacity they thought it right to challenge the encroachment of religious authority on their sphere of responsibility, for they argued that they had to reckon realistically with political existence and to deal faithfully with the world as it was and not as it ought to be.

---

[1] Cf. E. Sellin, *op. cit.*, pp. 206–7.
[2] G. von Rad, 'Die ältere Weisheit Israels', pp. 66–67. *Old Testament Theology* (tr. D. M. G. Stalker, 1962), i, 433–4.
[3] See below, Part Two.

III

ON THE DEFINITION OF OLD WISDOM

THIS brings us to the consideration of an 'old wisdom' of a different kind from that which I have been trying to describe. This old wisdom, according to von Rad,[1] is a blend of anthropocentricity and piety. Its *Sitz im Leben* was the court and its primary function the training of officials, but the 'fear of God' was an original ingredient of it. Thus in the Joseph story, which von Rad describes as old wisdom, Joseph is portrayed as a man who fears God.[2] My disagreement with von Rad does not hinge on the question whether these officials were religious or irreligious, but on whether the fear of God was an effective part of their wisdom. That this wisdom does not admit piety is to be accounted for by the fact that it is a wisdom of statecraft, that its practitioners have to take the world as they find it and that in their approach to its complex reality they do not permit themselves the luxury of religious or ethical assumptions.

In discussing this problem von Rad[3] envisages the *ḥāḵām* as a wisdom teacher rather than a statesman and he assumes that the question of a conflict between *ʿēṣā* and religious authority does not arise. His view is that the *ḥāḵām* operates in the most ordinary sphere of daily life and gives his advice in relation to the most humdrum matters. He is concerned not with divine commandments but with instructions derived from experience. Hence what he offers to young men is no more than *ʿēṣā* and as such does not demand obedience. It is to be compared to the summing-up of a judge to a jury; it appeals to the judgment of those who hear and makes decision easier.

On this view the danger of a conflict between *ʿēṣā* and the *dāḇār* of Yahweh does not arise, because this is a wisdom which prescribes limits to itself and which is positively related to the world

[1] G. von Rad, 'Josephgeschichte und ältere Chokma', *Supplement to VT* I (1953), pp. 120–7.

[2] Cf. also 'Die ältere Weisheit Israels', pp. 65–66, 71–72.

[3] *Ibid.*, pp. 66–67. *Theology*, pp. 433–5.

of the cult. Hence von Rad can say: 'In it [wisdom] two things were joined, that manly confidence in appropriating life and, at the same time, that knowledge of the boundaries set and the readiness to make shipwreck with all wisdom before God.'[1]

The Joseph story does not seem to me to be old wisdom, for it bears certain marks of the accommodation of wisdom to Israelite piety. This can be well seen in Gen. 41.25ff. Joseph interprets Pharaoh's dream (vv. 25–32) not because his technique is superior to the Egyptian specialists who were baffled by it (v. 8), but because he is charismatically endowed—the spirit of God is with him.[2] Joseph therefore, like Daniel, succeeds not because of his access to a body of esoteric knowledge on dream phenomena, but because of the illumination which he receives from God. In this respect the Joseph story participates in the Jewish reorientation of esoteric lore which I shall discuss below in connection with Daniel's role as a dream interpreter.[3]

Having interpreted Pharaoh's dream, Joseph makes practical proposals as to the action which should be taken to meet the situation which the dream predicts (vv. 33–36). He suggests that a man who is perspicacious (*nāḇōn*) and sagacious (*ḥāḵām*) should be set over the land of Egypt in order to implement this plan. Now, there is no reason to believe that Joseph has in mind a man who has the spirit of God and who can interpret dreams, since these are not the qualifications required by the person who is to implement Joseph's plan. What is needed is a first-class administrator and executive who has grasped what requires to be done and who has the drive to bring the plan to fruition, and the words *nāḇōn* and *ḥāḵām* suggest that it is such a man whom Joseph has in mind. There is therefore every reason for concluding that *'îš nāḇōn wᵉḥāḵām* alludes to someone who has been educated for high office and who has the intellectual virtues conferred by a rigorous educational discipline and by experience of affairs.[4]

This, however, is not how *nāḇōn* and *ḥāḵām* are understood by

[1] G. von Rad, *ibid.*, p. 71.

[2] Cf. E. L. Ehrlich, *Der Traum im Alten Testament* (1953), p. 122. Ehrlich describes Joseph as a dream interpreter endowed by God who declines to take the credit for interpreting dreams and ascribes it to God.

[3] See below, pp. 94ff.

[4] E. L. Ehrlich, *op. cit.*, p. 82 (cf. p. 74, n. 1), holds that vv. 33–36 are composite, that 33 is a variant of 34 and 34 of 35 (48). This would make no difference to the account which I have given of 41.25ff.

Pharaoh, who appears to trace to the spirit of God not only Joseph's ability to interpret dreams, but also the practical advice which he offers in vv. 33–36 (cf. 'all this' in v. 39). At any rate, there is no doubt that Pharaoh is represented as saying that the *'īš nāḇōn wᵉḥāḵām* who is required to organize Egypt against the years of famine must be one who is possessed of the spirit of God. Thus Pharaoh says: 'Since God has divulged (*hōḏīaʿ*) all this to you, there is none so *nāḇōn* and *ḥāḵām* as you are' (v. 39, cf. v. 25, *higgīḏ*). Pharaoh wants Joseph as an administrator, but it is represented that the first-class administrator—the man who is *nāḇōn* and *ḥāḵām*—is he who possesses the spirit of God. This is a reinterpretation of the vocabulary of old wisdom and an accommodation of it to Israelite piety. That is to say, the statesman no less than the interpreter of dreams must be charismatically endowed.[1]

Despite these particular difficulties which I feel in relation to the Joseph story, I believe that von Rad's concept of old wisdom deserves careful consideration and I propose now to enquire more closely what this concept is. We may begin with certain verses cited by von Rad[2] from the book of Proverbs. A man may plan the way ahead with his mind (*lēḇ*), but it is Yahweh who orders his step (16.9). A man's head (*lēḇ*) may be full of plans, but it is Yahweh's *ʿēṣā* which will be implemented (19.21). Since it is Yahweh who orders a man's steps, no one, however keen his mind, can see the way ahead (20.24). There is no wisdom (*ḥoḵmā*), no perspicacity (*tᵉḇūnā*), no counsel (*ʿēṣā*) over against Yahweh. The horse is harnessed for the day of battle, but the victory comes from Yahweh (21.30–31).

It would seem to be perfectly possible to understand these passages as a rejoinder to the claims of old wisdom as I have defined it. They would then represent an attempt to demonstrate that the empire of the mind which the *ḥᵃḵāmīm* have pegged out for themselves is illusory. It is Yahweh's *ʿēṣā* and not the *ʿēṣā* of the statesmen which will be implemented and the intellectual virtues on which they place such store mean nothing to Yahweh (19.21, 21.30–31). Von Rad, however, may be right in supposing that the significance of these passages is that the rational or empirical

[1] See below, Part Two.

[2] G. von Rad, 'Josephgeschichte und ältere Chokma', pp. 124f. 'Die ältere Weisheit Israels', p. 70. *Theology*, p. 439.

tradition of wisdom in Israel prescribed limits for itself and 'always reckoned with God as a limiting factor and as incalculable'.[1] In this connection von Rad comments: 'What more could they (the wise men) have done theologically than keep setting up these sombre signs on the frontiers of this area? This last-mentioned group of maxims gives an extraordinary glimpse into the intention and insight of these teachers. They are aware that the area which man can grasp with his rational powers (*ratio*) and fill out with his being is really small. Wherever he turns, before he is aware of it, he is once more confronted with the perfectly incalculable element in the action of Jahweh. It is affecting to see how such a vital art of mastering life is aware that it must halt at these frontiers—indeed, it even contrives to liquidate itself there, as the last-mentioned maxim so magnificently says (Prov. xxi.30). It combines two things—man's confidence in his ability to master life and at the same time, with all the wisdom in the world, an awareness of the frontiers and a preparedness to fail in the sight of God.'[2]

There is an affinity between this understanding of old wisdom and von Rad's analysis of the Joseph and Rebekah stories in the book of Genesis. With regard to the Rebekah narrative he notes[3] that it is characterized by a detailed interest in the workings of the human personality and urges that this is literary experimentation and the breaking of new ground. It marks an effort to explore the riches and many-sidedness of the human person and is a kind of psychological analysis nourished by the mental climate of the age of Solomon. The worldliness of this narrative is an indication that the real centre of interest is man and not God and so the story is about men—their passions, desires, motives and intrigues. As such it deals with a web of human action and interaction, is earthy in its flavour and mundane in its setting. All this, von Rad holds, represents the retreat of the divine or the sacred from the field of human action and so is expressive of a 'humanism'.

God does not intervene in this world of unfettered human action in any directly miraculous way and yet, although the narrative has no supernatural elements in this sense, God does in a quite mysterious and unintelligible way superintend and overrule the entire proceedings, and so, in the last analysis, this confused tangle

[1] G. von Rad, *Theology*, p. 439.
[2] G. von Rad, *Theology*, p. 440.
[3] G. von Rad, *Genesis*, pp. 248–55.

of human motives and action is amenable to God's guidance and control. Thus the same could be said of the Rebekah story as von Rad says of the Joseph story: 'It cannot be denied that already in the Joseph story there is a threat of a complete severance of divine and human actions, and that human action under the burden of the all-sufficiency of divine guidance is depressed to a perilous degree of insignificance.'[1]

Further von Rad alludes to the 'profaneness' of the expressions which are used to describe the guidance of Rebekah and says: 'They had to be profane, for at that time faith had no traditional forms of expression for such concealed, all-pervasive management by Yahweh. In contrast to the notion that Yahweh acted primarily in miracles, in the charisma of a leader or in a cultic event, this conception of faith was something quite new. It appears to have become vital only in the period of the Solomonic enlightenment.'[2] What seems to me to be uppermost in the Rebekah narrative is the idea of a 'sign' and von Rad agrees that this is so, but he maintains that it is not the kind of 'sign' 'which ancient, i.e. sacred piety which believed in miracles, was accustomed to obtain'.[3]

The courtesies at the well are the occasion for the giving of Yahweh's guidance to Abraham's servant. We may suppose that the servant himself made the decision to address Rebekah, perhaps influenced by her beauty. But for the rest he was not depending on his wits or judgment for the successful outcome of the affair; he was relying entirely on the *mal'āḵ* of Yahweh (Gen. 24.7). Thus in his prayer to Yahweh the servant makes a proposition and acts on the assumption that Yahweh has accepted it, believing that he will take control of the affair and bring it to fruition. This is, in fact, what happens, for Yahweh honours the 'sign' and the servant is brought to Abraham's brother's house and furnished with a bride for Isaac who will meet every desire of Abraham's heart.

I have some difficulty in accepting von Rad's opinion that the fear of God is the 'foundation on which the educational ideal of old wisdom rests'.[4] Mowinckel's[5] position is, in some respects,

[1] G. von Rad, 'Josephgeschichte und ältere Chokma', p. 125. *Genesis*, pp. 428–34. 'Die ältere Weisheit Israels', pp. 70–72.
[2] G. von Rad, *Genesis*, p. 255, cf. pp. 29ff.
[3] G. von Rad, *ibid*., p. 251.
[4] G. von Rad, *ibid*., p. 431.
[5] S. Mowinckel, 'Psalms and Wisdom' (Rowley Festschrift), pp. 207–8.

similar to that of von Rad. He says that the sages or scribes who were practitioners of wisdom all over the ancient Near East were men at court and diplomats in the foreign service of their respective countries, but he argues that, although their wisdom is utilitarian, it, nevertheless, has a religious basis. 'The true wisdom is the fear of God.' Yet, says Mowinckel, this wisdom literature is related to social position and profession and has a universal and rational character. It inculcates what, from the point of view of the ancient East, were universal, human virtues.

The emphasis on the fear of God and the hiddenness of God's guidance in the Joseph story or on the hiddenness of God's guidance and the 'sign' in the Rebekah story could be interpreted as a rejoinder to the old wisdom which I have tried to define and a denial of effective self-determination to the *ḥᵃḵāmîm*. God alone can take decisions and implement them. His ways are mysterious to men and the manner in which the divine action interacts with human actions cannot be shown. Nevertheless God's will is the ultimate reality and so the best of human plans are liable to be ineffective and to come unstuck. Certainly the 'sign', as a means of arriving at a decision, implies the invoking of the supernatural and is different in kind from the empirical processes of *'ēṣā*.[1] Then again I find it hard to accept that a concept of guidance in which the *mal'āḵ* of Yahweh plays a part is native to old wisdom.[2]

I have been discussing old wisdom in a much narrower context than von Rad and I have envisaged it as primarily a disciplined empiricism engaged with the problems of government and administration. Consequently the *ḥᵃḵāmîm* of whom I have been speaking were statesmen or officials. The serious question which I would ask is whether the kind of representation which von Rad discovers in the Joseph and Rebekah stories is compatible with the claims of such *ḥᵃḵāmîm* to conduct political affairs successfully by the employment of a strict empirical method. Even if von Rad is right in supposing that these men recognized a boundary or limit at which they had to surrender their empiricism to a fear of God, this is far from disposing of the possibility of a conflict between the empirical *'ēṣā* of statesmanship and the authoritative, revealed

[1] There is a similar employment of 'sign' in the books of Samuel. See W. McKane, *I and II Samuel* (Torch Bible Commentaries, 1963), on I.10.1ff.; 14.8–12; II.5.24.

[2] On the *mal'āḵ* of Yahweh as the agent of divine guidance see below, pp. 58ff.

dāḇār of Yahweh which addresses itself to the field of political decision. There will be no agreement as to where the boundary is to be drawn. Those who speak Yahweh's *dāḇār* will claim for it nothing less than the total life of Israel; they will say that such total guidance by a revealed authoritative word has always been the way in Israel. They will refuse to acquiesce in a situation where the questions which affect most profoundly the life of the nation are resolved by the procedures of an empirical *'ēṣā*. The statesman as a *ḥāḵām* may, as von Rad supposes, recognize a boundary at which he confronts God and where his disciplined empiricism must give place to the fear of God, but he will not accept that this boundary line should be drawn inside the area of statesmanship.

Duesberg comes nearer to the heart of the matter when he says: 'If there is not a permanent contradiction between the requirements of the fear of God, of justice and repentance, on the one part, and the assiduous industry of the life of the court, of diplomacy and of the royal treasury on the other, the harmony between the demands of conscience and the service of the master is not constant.'[1] Duesberg, however, supposes that the 'scribes' addressed themselves to the task of constructing a theory of success which would be subordinate to the Yahwistic ethic, and so he apparently believes that the Israelite statesmen (*ḥᵃḵāmīm*) tried from the outset to incorporate the fear of Yahweh into their system. With Duesberg's remark[2] that the 'scribes' were not necessarily irreligious I agree, but this is not the same thing as the assertion that the fear of Yahweh was a constituent part of the *'ēṣā* which regulated their approach to statecraft.

[1] H. Duesberg, *op. cit.*, i, p. 456.
[2] H. Duesberg, *ibid.*, p. 232.

IV

THE CASE OF AHITHOPHEL

I RETURN to Ahithophel[1] and to II Sam. 16.23, which reads: 'And the advice (*'ēṣā*) of Ahithophel which he gave in those days was as if one should ask concerning the word (*dāḇār*) of God. Thus was all the advice (*'ēṣā*) which Ahithophel gave to both David and Absalom.' Taken at its face value[2] the verse means that there are two parallel and unconnected systems of reliable guidance in matters of state; on the one hand there is *'ēṣā* and on the other there is the *dāḇār* of God. That *'ēṣā* in this verse does refer specifically to political advice or policy is indicated by its association with the names of David and Absalom ('Thus was all the *'ēṣā* which Ahithophel gave both to David and Absalom') and by the circumstance that Ahithophel was a *yō'ēṣ* like Ahikar and held high office under David.[3] In virtue of his influential role as an adviser and policy-maker and the reputation for sagacity which he enjoyed he can certainly be classed as both a *sōp̄ēr* and a *ḥāḵām*.[4] II Sam. 16.23 throws an interesting light on the practical wisdom of statesmanship and von Rad[5] has described the Ahithophel episode as a *locus classicus* for the elucidation of the sphere of *'ēṣā*. *Dāḇār* in this verse may be thought to refer to the utterance of a prophet or to the decision of the oracle, but, in either case, the according of equal status to *'ēṣā* and *dāḇār* should be contrasted with the attitude revealed in the prophetic polemic against *'ēṣā* where the incompatibility of the rival claims of *'ēṣā* and *dāḇār* in relation to crucial matters of political policy is expressly maintained.[6]

II Sam. 16.23 represents that there are two sources of political guidance available to the king in Israel. On the one hand there is

[1] See above, p. 13.
[2] See above, p. 13.
[3] See above, pp. 17–18.
[4] Cf. H. Duesberg, *op. cit.*, i, p. 220. Duesberg formulates the equation 'scribe' = sage = counsellor.
[5] G. von Rad, 'Die ältere Weisheit Israels', p. 64. *Theology*, p. 431.
[6] See below, Part Two.

the revealed word of the prophet[1] or the verdict of the priestly oracle (Urim and Thummim) and on the other there is a guidance which is a purely human product and is the fruit of empirical sagacity. These two systems are entirely separate and disconnected and it is said of Ahithophel that his shrewdness and perspicacity are such that his *ʿēṣā* has the same quality of inerrancy as the prophetic *dāḇār* or the decision of the priestly oracle. In this connection Noth[2] observes that the concept of wisdom in the narratives about David, Absalom and Ahithophel reflects the intellectual climate of the age of Solomon. The *ʿēṣā* which brings success is that of the sagacious statesman, and failure to heed it brings such consequences as are comparable with those resulting from a failure to obey God. God is represented as controlling history through the mediation of human decisions; that is, to neglect *ʿēṣā* is to be exposed to the judgment of God.

When we look at the books of Samuel we find that David is represented as resorting to the oracle[3] in order to obtain decisive guidance in relation to important political and military decisions. I have argued elsewhere that the point of view of I Sam. 22[4] is that a king who has been rejected by a prophet of Yahweh and who has extirpated the legitimate priestly house has no future in Israel. The presupposition of this representation is that the king, if he is to govern wisely and to take the right political and military decisions, must have regular access to Yahweh's guidance, and this assumes a solidarity of king and priest, since the priest is the custodian of the oracle. In this connection it should be noted that after the massacre at Nob David is joined by the only survivor of the priestly house of Eli, and Abiathar's solidarity with David is a portent that the future lies with him—a king whose rule will have the support of a legitimate priesthood.

Hence the occasions on which David seeks divine guidance in I Sam. 23 and elsewhere are connected with his acquisition of Abiathar and the ephod. The procedure followed with Urim and Thummim is indicated clearly in I Sam. 14.41–42 (following the longer text of the Greek in v. 41): 'And Saul said to Yahweh: "O

[1] Cf. I Sam. 22.5.

[2] M. Noth, 'Die Bewährung von Salomos "Göttlicher Weisheit" ', pp. 236–7.

[3] The lot was one among many oracular techniques in use in Babylonia and Assyria. B. Meissner, *op. cit.*, ii, pp. 267–75.

[4] W. McKane, *I and II Samuel, in loc.*

God of Israel, why do you not answer your servant this day? If this iniquity is in me or in Jonathan, my son, give Urim, but, if this iniquity is in your people Israel, give Thummim." And Jonathan and Saul were taken and the people excluded. And Saul said: "Cast between me and Jonathan, my son." And Jonathan was taken.'[1] A case of David's use of Abiathar and the ephod is I Sam. 30.7–8, where he receives a reassuring answer to a crucial question: Should he pursue the Amalekites? Here he may be asking implicitly whether the Amalekites have already slaughtered the wives and children. At any rate, the notice in v. 2 that the Amalekites had killed no one is evidently intended to register a providential circumstance which enables David to restore what might have been a hopeless situation.[2]

Here, then, is one respect in which David is no longer at a disadvantage *vis-à-vis* Saul, who now has no access to Yahweh's guidance. Saul's decision to engage the services of a necromancer in I Sam. 28 is the consequence of this lack of guidance. He is subject to severe Philistine pressure and, when he asks for advice from Yahweh, none is forthcoming. So he seeks illumination through the medium of dreams and follows the oracular procedure laid down for Urim and Thummim, but Yahweh is silent. He then takes steps to consult the ghost of Samuel, but no word of comfort comes to him from the world of the dead.[3]

But David is also represented as acknowledging the *'ēṣā* of Ahithophel as a reliable source of political guidance, and he himself takes up a realistic and earthy attitude to the situation created by Absalom's *coup d'état* and determines to employ every resource of statecraft and espionage in order to counter the sagacity of Ahithophel. He is convinced that the presence of Ahithophel on Absalom's side greatly increases the gravity of his own position (II Sam. 15.31), for Ahithophel is a seasoned statesman who will give Absalom the very best *'ēṣā*. Consequently David is anxious to nullify the *'ēṣā* of Ahithophel and this he does by planting Hushai within Absalom's council of war (II Sam. 15.34).

He takes this action because he is afraid that Ahithophel, for whose weight and prestige as a political and military adviser he has

[1] For Saul's use of Urim and Thummim see further I Sam. 14.36–37.
[2] For David's use of Urim and Thummim see further II Sam. 5.19, 23; 21.1.
[3] See W. McKane, *op. cit., in loc.*

the healthiest respect, will dominate Absalom's war cabinet and have no difficulty in getting his policies accepted. He hopes that if an adviser of Hushai's eminence[1] is present and is playing his game, he may be able to negative the *'ēṣā* of Ahithophel. And so, although David says that it is Yahweh who will decide the issue, he, nevertheless, uses every trick of statecraft to frustrate Absalom's designs and ensure the victory of his cause.

Further the account of the rejection of Ahithophel's advice is in accord with the representation of II Sam. 16.23 that *'ēṣā* is a self-contained system of political wisdom. If Yahweh is not on Absalom's side (II Sam. 17.14) and if Ahithophel (whose *'ēṣā* is as if one should ask concerning the *dāḇār* of Yahweh) is, a stalemate exists. In what way can Yahweh intervene so as to invalidate the *'ēṣā* of Ahithophel? The answer to this question is found not in a miraculous intervention, but in the lack of intellectual discrimination among those who have to decide between the competing policies of Ahithophel and Hushai.

Ahithophel's *'ēṣā* is marked by psychological astuteness and brilliant simplicity. Hushai sets out to darken counsel and give bad advice, and he succeeds in his aim. The real fools are Absalom and the elders of Israel who cannot distinguish between a bold and serious plan and a bogus strategy. The irony of Absalom's case was that he rested his cause on the sagacity of his professional advisers and that he had one such adviser whose judgment was impeccable, but that neither he nor the elders of Israel[2] had the critical astuteness to distinguish between wisdom and folly. It was by exploiting this circumstance that Yahweh defeated the *'ēṣā* of Ahithophel (II Sam. 17.4).

Three other passages which presuppose a dualism akin to that of *'ēṣā* and *dāḇār* are II Sam. 14.17, 20 and 19.28 [27]. In 14.17 David is said to be as wise as the messenger (or 'angel') of God to hear good

[1] See above, p. 18.

[2] In connection with the briefing of the elders by the two professional advisers, Ahithophel and Hushai, note the office of *rabiānum* in Babylonia mentioned by B. Meissner, *op. cit.*, i, pp. 120–1. The *rabiānum* stood at the head of the civic administration. As the highest judge he decided the most important legal questions and guided the deliberations of the elders. Cf. Ezek. 7.26, according to which *'ēṣā* is the business of the elders. J. Fichtner, 'Jesaja unter den Weisen', col. 77, suggests that the *ḥakāmīm*, who were politically influential in the pre-exilic period, may have subsequently declined in importance and left the field to the elders. See W. McKane, *I and II Samuel*, on II Sam. 17.4. Also J. L. McKenzie, 'The Elders in the Old Testament', *Biblica* 40 (1959), pp. 532ff.

and evil. 'Hear' is legal terminology and the woman is expressing her confidence that David will 'hear' the case and so sift the evidence as to arrive at a sound judgment (cf. v. 8, where 'I shall give orders concerning you' means 'I shall make an order concerning you', i.e. 'I shall set in motion the machinery which will implement my verdict concerning you'—another piece of legal terminology). II Sam. 14.17 then refers particularly to David's legal acumen and to his skill in sifting the evidence and this is the sense in which Solomon is wise in I Kings 3.16ff.

Similarly where Mephibosheth says of David in II Sam. 19.28 [27] that he is like the messenger (or 'angel') of God he is expressing the confidence that David will not be fooled by the misrepresentation of Ziba, but will get to the bottom of the affair and separate truth from falsehood. David's decision to share the estate between them (v. 30 [29]) probably reflects his conclusion that there was no possibility of ascertaining which of them was telling the truth.

II Sam. 14.20, on the other hand, refers rather to David's shrewd and penetrating mind and to his knack of ferreting out the truth in tracing his interview with the woman to its ultimate source in Joab's efforts to influence a major policy decision.[1] But in all three passages 'my lord is as wise as the *mal'āḵ* of God' exhibits a dualism similar to that of *'ēṣā* and *dāḇār* in II Sam. 16.23. David's *ḥoḵmā* lies in his ability to use his native wits, in his qualities as a hard and clear thinker and in the delicacy of his appraisal David's wisdom and the wisdom of the *mal'āḵ* of God are assumed to be two separate and parallel systems of wisdom, each with its own distinctive procedures, the one relying on human reason and the other on a divine revelation communicated by the *mal'āḵ* of God. But the two 'ways', although they are distinct from each other, are represented as equal in respect of luminosity and utter dependability.

That this is a correct understanding of the reference to the *mal'āḵ* of God in these passages and that the antithesis of *mal'āḵ* of God and *ḥōḵmā* in these passages is akin to that of *dāḇār* (of God) and *'ēṣā* is confirmed by those other Old Testament passages where the *mal'āḵ* of Yahweh or the *mal'āḵ* of God is the one who speaks

[1] I have tried to show elsewhere that Joab is portrayed as a skilful exponent of the art of statesmanship, a master of *'ēṣā*. See *I and II Samuel* on II.11.16–17; 14 and 18–19.

the word of God.[1] Among these passages are two which are of special interest. In one the prophet Haggai is called the *mal'āḵ* of Yahweh who speaks the message (*mal'ᵃḵûṯ*) of Yahweh to the people (Hag. 1.13). Here *mal'aḵûṯ YHWH* is to be equated with the *dāḇār* which the prophet speaks.[2] The other passage (Mal. 2.7) states that the lips of the priests should guard knowledge (*daʿaṯ*) and that men seek instruction (*tôrā*) from his mouth, for he is the *mal'āḵ* of Yahweh of Hosts. We can see here the connection between 'lips' and 'mouth' and the priestly office of *mal'āḵ YHWH*. That is to say the priest *qua mal'āḵ YHWH* should be Yahweh's spokesman (should speak his *dāḇār*) and impart authoritative instruction to the people.

The dualism of *ʿēṣā* and *dāḇār* which is set out in II Sam. 16.23 should not be regarded as a propagandist inflation of the prestige of *ʿēṣā*. It appears in a book where, as I have shown, the oracle is represented as having a decisive role in the eliciting of political and military decisions. The revealed word of God, according to the representation of the books of Samuel, exercises a decisive influence on statesmanship. It is not therefore the point of view of the *ḥᵃḵāmîm* (or *sôpᵉrîm* or *śārîm*) which is being pushed, for they would have been unwilling to concede that the *dāḇār* of God—the authoritative revealed word—was such a major factor in statesmanship. II Sam. 16.23, which implies that the *dāḇār* of God and *ʿēṣā* are equal partners in statecraft, is not, then, the voice of the *ḥᵃḵāmîm*. They would not have conceded this point, not because they were fundamentally irreligious, but because they did not

[1] Gen. 16.7, 9, 10, 11: the angel of Yahweh communicates Yahweh's word to Hagar. Gen. 21.17–18: the angel of God speaks to Hagar. Gen. 22.15–18: the angel of Yahweh reveals Yahweh's word to Abraham. Gen. 31.11–13: the angel of God speaks to Jacob in a dream. Judg. 2.1–4: the angel of Yahweh speaks Yahweh's word to all the people of Israel. Judg. 5.23: the angel of Yahweh commands a curse against Meroz. Judg. 6.11ff.: the angel of Yahweh speaks Yahweh's word to Gideon. Judg. 13.3–5, 13–14: the angel of Yahweh speaks to Manoah and his wife and promises her a son. I Kings 13.18: the anonymous prophet of Bethel says to the man of God: 'I too am a prophet as you are and a *mal'āḵ* spoke to me by the *dāḇār* of Yahweh . . .' I Kings 19.7; II Kings 1.3, 15: the angel of Yahweh brings Yahweh's word to Elijah the prophet. I Chron. 21.18: the angel of Yahweh delivers a word to Gad, the prophet, which he is to communicate to David. Notice that the *mal'āḵ* in Zechariah (1.9, 13, 14; 2.2 [1.19]; 2.7 [3]; 4.1, 5; 5.10; 6.4, 5) approximates to the angelic interpreter of the later apocalyptic literature.

[2] Cf. Isa. 42.19, where the servant of Yahweh is called *mal'āḵî* ('my messenger'). This is the form of the name 'Malachi' and it designates the prophet as a *mal'āḵ* of Yahweh (cf. Mal. 3.1). L. Köhler, *Lexicon, s.v. mal'āḵî*. Cf. J. Lindblom, *Prophecy in Ancient Israel* (1962), p. 112.

believe that it was possible to confront the realities of government honestly or effectively from a posture of religious faith or passionate ethical commitment. The practice of statecraft as they understood it was a critical, rational activity, and this openness and scorn of all doctrinaire assumptions could not be combined with a reliance on supernatural guidance in matters of state.

The equation of *ʿēṣā* with the *dāḇār* of God in II Sam. 16.23 argues a situation in which *ʿēṣā* occupied a position of great strength and I have tried to show that there are features of the portrayal of events in the books of Samuel which indicate that the arts and skills of statecraft were highly regarded. *ʿēṣā* was influential in high places; the king was dependent on it and it dominated his policy-making. No attempt is made in the books of Samuel to demonstrate the interrelatedness of these two systems of guidance. It could be supposed that supernatural guidance through the oracle or the word of a prophet and empirical wisdom are parallel but unrelated ways leading to the same goal and that the decision which sagacity dictates somehow coincides with the guidance given by the revealed word of God. If this is so, however, it is not a fact which can be explained. It is unintelligible to us and in its presence we can only throw up our hands in wonder. The only point which seems to me to be worth making is that the *ḥ*ᵃ*ḵāmîm* would not make room for the *dāḇār* of God within the area of statesmanship. As statesmen they were empiricists and nothing else and they would have regarded it as a failure of professional integrity to allow piety to influence their public decisions. Wherever the boundaries of empiricism were drawn by the *ḥ*ᵃ*ḵāmîm*, the line did not run inside the area of statesmanship.

What this dualism of *ʿēṣā* and *dāḇār* really points to is a state of uneasy co-existence which falls to be resolved at a future date. This temporary and unsatisfactory truce will not last and we are to expect that the battle will be joined with *ʿēṣā* by those who are determined that the *dāḇār* of Yahweh shall be effectively asserted in every department of the life of the nation. For this elusive either-or formula really settles nothing and we may suspect that it reflects the practical predominance of *ʿēṣā*. But the prophets, who are the bearers of the *dāḇār* of Yahweh, will not remain for ever satisfied with this monopoly of *ʿēṣā* in the most crucial and far-reaching decisions which confront the nation, for this would seem to condemn them to ineffectiveness and even impotence, since it appears that the authority of Yahweh's *dāḇār* which they proclaim is to be acknowledged only where the consequences of such acknowledgment are harmless or of small effect. As prophets they are allowed to deal in small change, but they must leave the big business to the professional politicians. They can potter about in the backwaters of the nation's life, but they must not raise their voice in the capital and become involved in urgent political realities.

PART TWO

THE PROPHETIC USE OF THE VOCABULARY OF WISDOM

V

THE ATTACK ON OLD WISDOM[1]

Isaiah 5.19–24

ALTHOUGH Lindblom[2] argues that *ḥᵃkāmîm* in v. 21 does not refer particularly to a class of sages, I am satisfied that the vocabulary of these verses supports the probability of the opposite conclusion. Those who are attacked by the prophet say: 'Let him speed up and expedite his action (*maʿᵃśe*) that we may see, and let the policy (*ʿēṣā*) of the holy one of Israel draw near and arrive that we may know.' This is the voice of the statesmen of Judah whose business it is to make policy and who challenge the reality of the prophet's claim that it is Yahweh alone who shapes history—that policy and action belong to him alone.[3]

The unmistakable reference to the ethical neutrality of old wisdom is another aspect of the passage which points to the same conclusion. Thus v. 20 reads: 'Woe to those who name evil good and good evil; who make darkness light and light darkness, bitter sweet and sweet bitter.' This reflects the passionate ethical commitment of the prophet and his dislike of the flexibility of old wisdom. He thus goes so far as to assert that this produces a total perversion of moral judgment. Related to this is the attack on the corruption of the judiciary through the employment of bribes (v. 23), and in this connection it should be noted that there are wisdom sentences which recommend bribery as an item of practical wisdom.[4]

The most fundamental part of the indictment relates to the claims of these sages to be wise independent of Yahweh and the *dāḇār* of Yahweh, and to their mental posture as practitioners of a self-contained system of political wisdom.[5] They rely exclusively on rational scrutiny and on a practised delicacy of appraisal and

[1] Cf. J. Fichtner, 'Jesaja unter den Weisen', cols. 77–78.
[2] J. Lindblom, 'Wisdom in the Old Testament Prophets', p. 193. Cf. J. Fichtner, 'Jesaja unter den Weisen', col. 77–78.
[3] See below, pp. 79ff.
[4] Prov. 17.8, 19.6, 21.14.
[5] See above, pp. 46ff.

have no room in their system for the religious authority which is exemplified in the prophetic *dāḇār*. Hence the prophet says: 'Woe to those who are *ḥakāmîm* in their own eyes and are far-seeing (*neḇōnîm*) in their own estimation' (v. 21), and then goes on to assert that they have rejected Yahweh's instruction (*tōrā*) and have spurned the utterance (*'imrā*) of the holy one of Israel (v. 24). Verse 21 is one of the phrases adduced by Fichtner[1] in order to establish Isaiah's connections with the wisdom tradition. Notice, however, how Isaiah turns the phrase against the wise and the pretensions of wisdom. It is not now the fool (Prov. 26.5, 12) nor the sluggard (Prov. 26.16) nor the rich man who is not *mēḇîn* (Prov. 28.11), who is *ḥāḵām be'ēnāw*, but the sage himself. In opposing the *dāḇār* of Yahweh to *'ēṣā* Isaiah is nearer to the point of view of Prov. 3.7, where the meaning of 'wise in your own eyes' is significantly changed. 'Be not wise in your own eyes, fear Yahweh and turn away from evil.'

Isa. 5.19–24 illustrates the close connection between *'ēṣā* and action (*ma'aśe*) and so the aptness of the translation 'policy'. Fichtner[2] makes too sharp a separation between the two meanings which he assigns to *'ēṣā*, 'advice' and 'plan', although he does say that the two meanings are related in so far as the adviser formulates a plan which becomes a firm decision on which action is to be based. The translation 'policy' has the effect of minimizing this distinction between 'advice' and 'plan' which Fichtner presses, for 'policy' indicates that *'ēṣā* is advice with a view to action. The conclusions which Fichtner draws are not altogether acceptable to me and, in particular, I do not agree that Isaiah uses *y'ṣ* and *'ēṣā* differently from the author of the Ahithophel passage.[3] It is misleading to say that in the latter *y'ṣ* and *'ēṣā* mean 'advise' and 'advice' respectively, while the prophet uses them in the sense of 'to plan' and 'plan'. What Isaiah is really doing is to claim for Yahweh exclusively the *'ēṣā* of which such *ḥakāmîm* or *yō'aṣîm* as Ahithophel were the professional dispensers.

Fichtner is nevertheless aware that Isaiah is opposing the *'ēṣā* of Yahweh to the *'ēṣā* of men and that his words are directed particularly against foreign alliances.[4] He is saying that only Yahweh's

[1] J. Fichtner, 'Jesaja unter den Weisen', col. 78.
[2] J. Fichtner, 'Jahves Plan in der Botschaft des Jesaja', *ZAW* 63 (1951), p. 18.
[3] See above, pp. 55ff.
[4] J. Fichtner, *op. cit.*, pp. 26–27.

ʿēṣā will be implemented (*tāqūm, tihye*).[1] What Fichtner seems to me to miss is the fact that Isaiah is using the vocabulary of wisdom in order to refute the claims of its practitioners in Judah, and his opinion that Isaiah is using *yʿṣ* and *ʿēṣā* in a special sense has the effect of hiding from him that the prophet is trying to wrest *ʿēṣā* from the *ḥᵃḵāmīm* and to exhibit it as an exclusive activity of Yahweh.[2]

The test of *ʿēṣā* is its effectiveness as policy and this presupposes that those who formulate it should have the energy and power (*kōaḥ, gᵉḇūrā*) to effect its successful implementation. Thus we shall find that the recurrence of this collocation of *ʿēṣā* and *kōaḥ* or *gᵉḇūrā* is a key to the inner character of the controversy between prophet and statesman. What it reflects primarily, however, is the practical and dynamic bent of old wisdom, and there are a few other passages which make this same point.

In Isa. 7.5 *yʿṣ* is used of the policy of Syria and Ephraim to attack and subjugate Judah, and in Isa. 36.5 we read: 'Do you think (reading *'āmartā*) mere words are policy (*ʿēṣā*) and power (*gᵉḇūrā*) for war?' That is, the acid test of *ʿēṣā* is the degree of success which it achieves when it is put into operation and so there is little profit in spending time over *ʿēṣā*, unless one possesses *gᵉḇūrā* to give effect to it. Hence it is an activity proper to men who *really* have power and responsibility. There is a similar combination of *ḥoḵmā* and *gᵉḇūrā* in Jer. 9.22 [23]. The *ḥāḵām* is not to glory in his *ḥoḵmā* nor the strong man in his *gᵉḇūrā*. The connection between *ʿēṣā* and the political planning or calculation which goes into policy-making is further seen in Jer. 49.30. The inhabitants of Hazor are to flee, because Nebuchudrezzar has made (*yʿṣ*) a policy (*ʿēṣā*) and worked out (*ḥšb*) a plan (*maḥᵃšāḇā*)[3] against them.

The same practical bent is characteristic of *śkl*,[4] as can be seen from I Sam. 18.5, 14–15, 30 and Jer. 20.11. David acts with aptitude (*yaśkīl*) wherever Saul sends him on military duty and so his promotion to supreme command is generally approved. He is more competent (*śāḵal*; BH conjectures *maśkīl*) in warfare against

[1] *Ibid.*, p. 22, n. 25.

[2] See below, pp. 79ff.

[3] Cf. H. Duesberg, *op. cit.*, i, p. 252. Duesberg says that a *maḥᵃšāḇā* is an action which is carefully calculated.

[4] Cf. H. Duesberg, *ibid.*, pp. 249–50. *škl* means 'prudent' and includes the success which is the reward of prudence.

the Philistines than all his professional colleagues. David is a *maśkīl* in the sense that he displays competence and proves effective as a man of action. Similarly the Jeremiah passage alludes to the incompetence or ineptness of the prophet's pursuers (*lō' hiśkīlū*).

Isaiah 10.13ff.

These verses describe the ambitious political and military policies of the King of Assyria and his colossal confidence in his own capacity and power. He has hewn out an empire for himself by the strength (*kōaḥ*) of his hand and by his wisdom (*ḥoḵmā*), for he is perspicacious (or 'he has good judgment', *nᵉḇūnōṯī*). *ḥkm*[1] and *bīn*[2] are thus used of aptitude for government and ability to build an empire, and are, in this connection, associated with *kōaḥ*. This is therefore the practical wisdom and grasp which goes hand in hand with action, and its function is not only to make right decisions but to carry them out with energy and incisiveness once they have been made.

The prophet vigorously repudiates the all-embracing claims of this science of government. It is not, after all, emperors and statesmen who move the world and the resolute humanism of their hard-thinking posture does not win for them a monopoly in the world of politics as they suppose it does. It is not they but Yahweh who shapes history; it is he who takes the big decisions and implements them, and so the prophet as the bearer of the *dāḇār* which divulges Yahweh's *'ēṣā* is a key political figure.

The relation of this to the doctrine of 'instrumentality' which the prophet applies to Assyria is evident from a comparison of 10.5–11 with 10.15. The rulers of Assyria suppose that they are in complete control and that as they proceed with their plan for conquest and empire they are demonstrating that they have the power to impose their will on events (especially 10.7, where *yᵉḏamme*, 'deliberate' and *yaḥšōḇ*, 'calculate', occur in association with *lēḇāḇ*, which should be translated 'mind').[3] The prophet asserts that Assyria is no more than a rod in Yahweh's hand which he is wield-

[1] Cf. H. Duesberg, *op. cit.*, i, p. 240.

[2] Cf. H. Duesberg, *ibid.*, pp. 245–8. *Bīn* has the greatest intellectual content of all the Hebrew vocabulary of wisdom. It refers to the turning over of every aspect of a problem and is the distinctive faculty of a reasonable man.

[3] See above, pp. 15–16. Cf. J. Fichtner, 'Jahves Plan in der Botschaft des Jesaja', p. 24.

ing in order to implement his own distinctive policy, that is, in order to make history amenable to morality and to bring to judgment those who do not pass this ethical test.

The reality of the situation, then, is that the policy by which the statesmen of Assyria set such store is not permitted by Yahweh to have any decisive influence on the pattern of history, and the power which they exercise is real only in so far as it is an extension of Yahweh's power. The absurdity of the situation then is that these statesmen suppose that they are absolutely independent agents and that their *ḥoḵmā* and *kōaḥ* are the only things in the world. 'Shall the axe boast itself over him who hews with it or shall the saw make itself greater than he who wields it? As if a staff were to wield him who raises it (reading *mᵉrīmō*) or a stick that which is not wood' (10.15). Hence when Yahweh has no further use for this staff and throws it away, the *ḥoḵmā* and *tᵉḇūnā* and *kōaḥ* which seemed so real to the statesmen of Assyria will dissolve into unreality.

Isaiah 19.11–13

The *śārīm* (who form the inner circle of Pharaoh's government and set themselves up as masters of *ʿēṣā*) are fools and Pharaoh's professional advisers have given idiotic advice.[1] The claim of these statesmen that they are *ben ḥᵃḵāmīm* probably means that they are accredited and properly qualified members of their profession who have come up through the recognized schools,[2] although it may allude to the operation of the hereditary principle in respect of high offices of state.[3] They also claim that their ancestry is royal (*ben malᵉḵē qeḏem*) and this Lindblom[4] connects with Ezek. 28.12ff., which means, in his opinion, that wisdom was first revealed to primeval Babylonian kings. Marti[5] observes that the Egyptian

[1] Reading *ḥᵃḵāmāw yāʿᵃṣū*. Without emending it is perhaps possible to translate: 'The wisest of Pharaoh's advisers are witless advice' (*ʿēṣā* abstract for concrete). So B. Duhm, *Jesaia* (HKAT, 1892); K. Marti, *Das Buch Jesaja* (KHKAT, 1900). O. Procksch, *Jesaja* I (KAT, 1930), suggests that *ḥaḵᵉmē* and *yōʿᵃṣē* are variants.

[2] See above, pp. 36ff.

[3] So Duhm and Marti. Also G. B. Gray, *Isaiah I–XXVII* (ICC, 1912). Cf. *Ahikar* i.10–12, ii.18 (A. E. Cowley, *op. cit.*, p. 212). Nadin is nominated by Ahikar as his successor and this is approved by Esarhaddon. See also the examples of the Egyptian 'Instruction' in A. Erman, *op. cit.*, pp. 54–85, and in *Ancient Near Eastern Texts* (ed. J. B. Pritchard), pp. 412ff.

[4] J. Lindblom, 'Wisdom in the Old Testament Prophets', p. 194.

[5] K. Marti, *op. cit., in loc.* Cf. O. Procksch.

royal family traced its descent from primeval kings, even from Re the sun-god and first King of Egypt, and that the highest offices of state, priestly and civil, were occupied by members of the royal family themselves.

If, then, these counsellors are so wise and perspicacious, let them divulge what Yahweh's policy is concerning (or 'against') Egypt.[1] These *ḥᵃḵāmîm* or *yōʿᵃṣîm* say that they are experts in *ʿēṣā*, but the prophet alleges that the statesmen of Egypt are fools who have led their country astray. 'The *śārîm* of Zoan (Tanis) are fools and those of Memphis are deluded. Those who were the cornerstones (reading *pinnōṯ*) of her tribes have led Egypt astray.'

Isaiah 29.14–16[2]

This passage alleges that the statesmen of Judah not only neglected to consult the prophet but engaged in cloak and dagger diplomacy and took pains to conceal the policy which they were pursuing. 'Woe to those who are secretive so as to conceal their *ʿēṣā* from Yahweh, whose activities are in the dark and who say: "Who sees us or is cognizant of us?" ' They are castigated by the prophet for their perverse and topsy-turvy thinking in language which recalls the attack on Assyria in 10.5ff. and the doctrine of instrumentality which is formulated there. The statesmen of Judah behave as if they were the potter and Yahweh the clay. It is as if an artifact should say of its maker: 'He did not make me'; or the object of art say of the artist: 'He has no insight.'

These pretensions are absurd, for those who indulge in them forget their creaturely status and suppose that they can behave towards Yahweh as if he were a creature. They use the grand terminology of wisdom in order to propagate their claims and describe the creative role which they suppose themselves to discharge. In truth they are not creative agents in history, nor do they exercise executive powers, and such words as *ʿēṣā*, *tᵉḇûnā* and *kōaḥ* can only properly be used of Yahweh himself, whether in view of the mental grasp and vast power revealed through his activities as

[1] Reading *wᵉyaggîḏû nāʾ lāḵ wᵉyōḏîʿû* with the Versions. Cf. J. Fichtner, 'Jahves Plan in der Botschaft des Jesaja', p. 23. Fichtner suggests that the representation of Yahweh as a *yōʿēṣ* formulating *ʿēṣā* in relation to the nations originated with Isaiah and was taken over by others in connection with foreign oracles.

[2] Cf. B. Gemser, *Sprüche Salomos* (HAT), p. 2. J. Lindblom, *op. cit.*, p. 194. J. Fichtner, *op. cit.*, p. 21.

creator of the world or because of his grand plan and power of enforcement in relation to history. So the ambitious vocabulary of wisdom belongs to him alone and the *ḥᵃḵāmīm* are deluded in their use of it. 'The wisdom of the *ḥᵃḵāmīm* will perish and the perspicacity of the *nᵉḇōnīm* will be hidden from view' (29.14).

Isaiah 30.1–5

This is an oracle of Yahweh uttered against rebellious children of whom it is said: 'They implement a policy (*ʿēṣā*) which does not derive from me and enter into an alliance (literally, "pour out a libation")[1] in which my spirit has no part.' This is directed against the statesmen of Judah who have concluded a pact with Egypt and have reposed the security of Judah in the strength of a powerful ally. Of such statesmen it is said: 'They did not enquire at my face', i.e. they did not seek Yahweh's *ʿēṣā*. This, in the context of a prophetic oracle, means that they did not ask the advice of Yahweh's prophet. The implication of this is that the only person with the credentials to make foreign policy is the prophet, because he is the bearer of the *dāḇār* which communicates Yahweh's *ʿēṣā*.

This passage is connected with the controversy between the prophet and the statesmen of Judah and its background is the claim of the latter that the rough and tumble of politics is not a seemly occupation for a man of God and should be left to those whose profession is diplomacy and whose political judgment has been acquired the hard way through many years of experience. These statesmen say in effect that what is required is a cool head and strong nerves and that only those who have given their lives to the art of politics can have the feel of delicate questions of home and foreign policy and the sense of timing which makes all the difference between success and failure.

The prophet, speaking for Yahweh, denies that statesmanship is such a pragmatic art and declares that it, too, belongs to Yahweh and to the prophet who speaks his word. It does not, after all, belong to the statesmen who pride themselves in their disciplined

[1] That is, the libation which seals a pact or alliance (so Duhm, Marti and Procksch). Procksch suggests further that the name of the deity would be invoked while the libation was being poured out and that the representatives of Judah would invoke the name of Yahweh. Yahweh, however, does not *really* participate in the pact or give it his assent. 'And not with my spirit' may mean 'not on the *ʿēṣā* of my prophet'. This makes it synonymous with the first member of the line (so Duhm and Procksch).

thinking and acute policy-making. The security of Judah is not to be found in foreign alliances but in a knowledge of Yahweh's *ʿēṣā* and obedience to its demands. It is vital for Judah to take cognizance of Yahweh's *ʿēṣā* and to align herself with it, for this will indubitably be implemented, whereas the professional politicians are deluded in imagining that their policies can shape the future. Since it is through the prophetic *dāḇār* that Yahweh's *ʿēṣā* is disclosed, statesmanship and policy-making are not the preserve of empirical politicians and, in fact, cannot be initiated with success, unless the unique contribution of the prophet is attended to at the outset.

Isaiah 31.1–3

These verses are directed against the presuppositions of the pact with Egypt, namely, that power is to be equated with armaments and that Judah's security can best be reposed in the horses and chariots of Egypt. It is not accidental that statesmen who think in this way should embark on their policies without asking Yahweh's advice.[1] Yet Yahweh, too, is a *ḥāḵām*[2] wielding power superior in kind to the armed might available to the *ḥᵃḵāmîm* of Egypt. Only his punitive resources (*wayyāḇēʾ rāʿ* or *wᵉyāḇēʾ rāʿ*) by which he implements[3] his words are in the service of morality and are directed against evildoers and the help offered by those who work evil (alluding to Judah's reliance on Egypt for help). Here material power (*bāśār*), that is, armament (*wᵉsûsēhem*) is contrasted with a spiritual power (*rûaḥ*) which belongs uniquely to God. When Yahweh decides to act (stretches out his hand [sc. for action]) he will make an end of the gross power of Egypt and, because Israel has sought help and security there, she, too, will fall beneath Yahweh's power.

So the hard-headed statesmen are not after all the realists they think they are, because the coarse power on which they rely is not the last word in the shaping of history. There is a higher spiritual power exercised directly by Yahweh and this makes nonsense of

[1] Cf. above, pp. 55ff., on II Sam. 16.23.

[2] I do not here follow the suggestion of M. Noth, 'Die Bewährung von Salomos "Göttlicher Weisheit" ', p. 232, that the reference to Yahweh as a *ḥāḵām* is probably ironical. Cf. J. Fichtner, 'Jesaja unter den Weisen', col. 80.

[3] *Lōʾ hēsîr* is the equivalent of *qûm* and *ʿmd* which are used elsewhere (Isa. 8.10, 14.24; Jer. 23.20; Ps. 33.9, 11).

all the calculations of the statesmen and their jockeying after power alliances.[1]

Jeremiah 49.7

The prophetic *dāḇār* is set against the political calculations of the *ḥᵃḵāmîm* in Edom,[2] and Yahweh, through the prophet, asserts that, when the threat of judgment against Edom has been fulfilled (vv. 8ff.), it will be seen that the *ḥᵃḵāmîm*, for all their pretensions, are incapable of imposing their purpose and will on the future or of contriving the security and prosperity of Edom. In that day the *ḥᵃḵāmîm* will be a sitting target for satire and the question will be asked:

> Has policy (*ʿēṣā*)[3] perished among the perspicacious,[4]
> Has their wisdom gone rancid?[5]

With this should be compared Jer. 50.35ff., which contains a prophetic threat against the governing *élite* of Babylon—against the power and wealth of the establishment (v. 37). The grouping of *ḥᵃḵāmîm* with *śārîm* and *gibbōrîm* again illustrates the politically influential role of the *ḥᵃḵāmîm* and their place at the centre of government in a partnership of *ʿēṣā* and *kōaḥ* (similarly Jer. 51.57).

Ezekiel 28.2ff.

This passage is somewhat removed in tone from the others in this section, but it has sufficient in common with them to merit inclusion. The commentators[6] are agreed that vv. 11ff. contain a myth of the same parentage as the Paradise myth in Gen. 2 and 3, but with more marked mythological features, in which the King of Tyre (Ithobaal II, who was king during the great siege, 585–73 BC)

[1] Cf. J. Fichtner, 'Jahves Plan in der Botschaft des Jesaja', p. 22, on Isa. 8.10. Fichtner would delete *kî ʿimmānû ʾēl*. The verse would then read: 'Make (reading *ʿᵃśû*) a policy (*ʿēṣā*) but it will come to nothing. Speak a word but it will not be implemented.'

[2] Cf. R. H. Pfeiffer, 'Edomite Wisdom', *ZAW* 44 (1926), pp. 13–25. H. Gressmann, *Israels Spruchweisheit*, pp. 20–21.

[3] J. Lindblom, 'Wisdom in the Old Testament Prophets', p. 194.

[4] *mibbānîm* or perhaps *minnᵉḇōnîm* (*BH*).

[5] So L. Köhler, *Lexicon s.v. srḥ*.

[6] R. Kraetzschmar, *Das Buch Ezechiel* (HKAT, 1900). J. Herrmann, *Ezechiel*, KAT (1924). G. A. Cooke, *The Book of Ezekiel* (ICC, 1936). A. Bertholet, *Hesekiel* (HAT, 1936). Cf. J. L. McKenzie, 'Mythological Allusions in Ezekiel 28.12–18', *JBL* 75 (1956). McKenzie says that this is a piece of Hebrew tradition concerning the first man more mythological than the corresponding Genesis story.

is depicted as the *Urmensch* or Adam. He was in Eden, the garden of God, full of wisdom and beauty[1] (vv. 12–13); he was on the holy mountain of God strutting about[2] in the midst of the stones of fire, perfect (*tāmīm*) in all his ways from the day of his creation (vv. 14–15).

How did this king misuse his wisdom so that he ceased to be *tāmīm* and perversion (*ʿawlā*) was found in him? Why was he cast out as profane from the mountain of God and banished by the cherub[3] from the midst of the stones of fire (v. 16)? Because of the lawless lust for power (*ḥāmās*) stimulated by his extensive commercial operations[4] (vv. 16, 18). Verse 17 describes the *hubris* of a tycoon and the phrase *gāḇah libbᵉḵā* indicates that both *yᵒpī* and *yipʿā* are used of the failure of the king to respect human bounds and his attempt to blow himself up to divine dimensions (cf. v. 7). The (Babylonian) army, which will execute Yahweh's judgment against the King of Tyre, will draw their swords against the resplendence (*yᵒpī*) of his wisdom and will profane his lustre (*yipʿā*).[5] In failing to observe the limits of his creatureliness, and

[1] G. R. Driver, 'Ezekiel Linguistic and Textual Problems', *Biblica* 35 (1954), pp. 158–9. Driver reads *ḥōṯam* (so *BH*) instead of MT *ḥōṯēm* and *taḵnīṯ* for *toḵnīṯ* on the basis of the use of Babylonian *taknū, taknītu* as a descriptive term in the genitive. *kᵉlīl* then is also to be taken as a noun (Babylonian *kilīlu*, Syriac *klīlā*) with G. and S. 'Thou art a seal of perfection, full of wisdom, and a crown of beauty.' Driver adds: 'The prophet, using two Babylonian words characteristic of Nebuchudrezzar's period, describes the king of Tyre somewhat ironically as a perfect work of art, a carved seal or a diadem set with precious stones, in his royal splendour.'

[2] So G. R. Driver, *ibid.*, p. 59, who cites Arabic *taballaka fī masyihi*, 'he swaggered in his gait'.

[3] Following G. and omitting *mimšaḥ hassōḵēḵ* in v. 14 and *hassōḵēḵ* in v. 16. Cooke observes that *hassōḵēḵ* probably represents the assimilation of the cherub of Paradise to the cherubim of the ark (Ex. 25.20; 37.9; I Kings 8.7). According to MT of v. 14 and v. 16 the king is to be identified with the cherub, but the role of the cherubim in the Genesis narrative (3.24) is probably a better guide than the Masoretic vocalization. Read *ʾeṯ* in v. 14 and *wᵉʾibbaḏᵉḵā* in v. 16 with *BH*.

[4] Cooke supposes that *bᵉrōb rᵉḵullāṯᵉḵā . . . ḥāmās* should be deleted, but, in any case, the same idea is elsewhere expressed in the chapter as, for example, in v. 5: 'Through your many-sided wisdom, through your commercial operations you have amassed wealth and you have become arrogant because of your wealth.' Hence my argument is unaffected by this critical point, but if the verse is to be retained, *millēʾṯā* should be read with G. and S.

[5] Cf. T. H. Gaster, *Les études classiques* 62 (1950), p. 124. On the basis of the Ugaritic usage of *ypʿ* (see G. R. Driver, *Canaanite Myths and Legends*, pp. 78–79, 86–87) Gaster suggests *hubris* or 'upstart conduct' as a translation of *yipʿā* in Ezek. 28.17. Note especially *Baal* III*B.1 (Driver, pp. 78–79), 'Thou hast sprung up (*ypʿt*) in thine impiety.' In *Baal* V.iva.4, 5 (Driver, pp. 86–87) *ypʿ* is used of enemies 'rising up'. Gaster's suggestion, however, does not suit Ezek. 28.7 so well. 'They will profane thy *hubris*' is less apt than 'they will profane thy lustre'. G. R. Driver, 'Ezekiel Linguistic and Textual Problems', p. 158, takes *yipʿā* to mean 'pre-eminent position',

grasping at a lustre and resplendence which properly belong to God alone, the King of Tyre has polluted his wisdom (v. 17).

Cooke[1] seeks a Babylonian origin for the imagery of this myth both in respect of the holy mountain of God and the stones of fire. The latter he explains as precious stones which impart brilliance and splendour to the Babylonian Paradise. Yet Cooke does not rule out Phoenician or Canaanite mediation[2] and I believe that Herrmann[3] and Bertholet[4] are right in supposing that the interpretation should hinge on this assumption, although, doubtless, the mythical mountain of God is ultimately of Babylonian origin.[5] Perhaps, as Herrmann suggests, we have to reckon with a localizing of the Garden of God or the holy mountain of God in the Lebanon and, in that case, we should think of Mount Zaphon (*Mons Casius*) with Eissfeldt[6] and G. R. Driver.[7]

The localizing of the myth in the Lebanon goes some way towards explaining why the prophet should have applied it to the King of Tyre in the manner in which he has done. Cooke says: 'The king of Tyre like the king of the old myth will be driven from the garden on the sacred mountain.'[8] But should we not look for a more intrinsic connection between the King of Tyre and the

---

'pre-eminence' and cites Arabic *yafaʿa*, 'ascended', 'grew up', *wafʿun*, 'high building'. He rejects Gaster's 'upstart conduct', but does hold that the word has to do with height rather than brilliance. He thus associates *yipʿā* primarily with Tyre's eminent position 'rising from a spit of rock running into the sea' and secondarily with her commanding mercantile position among the cities of the ancient Near East. There is, however, the point that *ypʿ* does seem to be used with the sense 'shine' in biblical Hebrew (especially Job 3.4 where *tōpaʿ* is used with *nᵉhārā*, 'light').

[1] G. A. Cooke, *op. cit.*, on Ezek. 28.14.

[2] *Ibid.*, p. 315. 'The story belongs, no doubt, to the common stock of Semitic myths, some of them preserved in the Babylonian epics, some in the Phoenician traditions.'

[3] *Op. cit.*, on Ezek. 28.14.

[4] *Op. cit.*, on Ezek. 28.11–19. Cf. G. Fohrer, *Ezechiel* (HAT, 1955), p. 162. Fohrer leaves it an open question whether the myth is a Canaanite one enriched with Babylonian motifs or vice versa. M. H. Pope, *El in the Ugaritic Texts* (Supplements to *VT*, II, 1955), pp. 97ff. Pope finds allusions in the Ezekiel passage to a myth concerning the deposition of El from the Ugaritic pantheon—a myth which he reconstructs from allusions in the Ugaritic literature.

[5] So Herrmann.

[6] O. Eissfeldt, *Baal Zaphon* (1932), pp. 14, 18ff.

[7] G. R. Driver, *Canaanite Myths and Legends*, p. 21, n. 1. Cf. Isa. 14.13. The mountain in the recesses of the north (*ṣāpōn*) where the King of Assyria proposes to set up his residence is a place of assembly of the gods (*mōʿēd*). Bertholet, however, questions whether this mountain of assembly was originally *Mons Casius* and so *ṣāpōn* here is perhaps not to be equated with Mount Zaphon.

[8] *Op. cit.*, p. 315.

myth than such a statement presupposes? Kraetzschmar[1] has given us a valuable clue in suggesting that the 'mountain of God' may be an allusion to the name *Ṣūr*. That there is this connection of ideas is suggested directly by 28.2: 'I am God and I occupy God's seat in the heart of the seas.' Or: 'I am a god and I occupy the seat of the gods in the heart of the seas.' It is this sense of absolute security felt by the King of Tyre in his island fortress which prompts the prophet to equate him with the *Urmensch* in Paradise on the mountain of God. Hebrew *ṣūr* is usually translated 'rock' rather than 'mountain' (although *ṣūrīm*, 'crags' approximates to 'mountains' in the phrase *mērō'š ṣūrīm* in Num. 23.9), but the Aramaic and Arabic cognates certainly mean 'mountain' (*ṭūr*).[2]

Herrmann[3] suggests that 28.3 should be regarded as a detail of the myth which emerges more clearly in vv. 11ff. I do not think that it is possible to come to a firm decision about this, but I agree with Bertholet[4] and G. R. Driver[5] that the reference in v. 3 ('Behold you are wiser than Danel') is to the Ugaritic Danel. This king was both wise (he once used his wits to obtain from the divine craftsman Kathir-and-Khasis a magic bow and arrows for his son Aqhat)[6] and righteous (he judged the cause of the widow and tried the case of the orphan),[7] and he enjoyed an intimate relationship with Baal,[8] who is once called Zephon (*ṣpn*).[9] Hence Zephon, which is properly the mountain (*Mons Casius*) where Baal dwells, becomes an appellation of the god, and so the god who was Danel's mediator and by whose name he made incantations was the god of the holy mountain. To this extent we can trace in the extant

[1] *Op. cit.*, on Ezek. 28.2.

[2] Arabic *ṭūr* is a loan word from Aramaic or Syriac. Cf. A. Jeffery, *The Foreign Vocabulary of the Qur'ān* (1938), pp. 206–7.

[3] *Op. cit.*, on 28.3. Also G. Fohrer, *op. cit.*, p. 159. J. L. McKenzie, *op. cit.*, p. 325, denies that Ezek. 28.1–10 and 12–18 form 'a single mythological complex'.

[4] *Op. cit.*, on 28.3. Bertholet points out that Danel is mentioned in Ezek. 14.14, 20 and that his appearance there between Noah and Job is an indication that he is not to be identified with the Daniel of the book of Daniel. He is not portrayed as a contemporary or near contemporary of Ezekiel, but as one of the three righteous men of Hebrew tradition.

[5] *Canaanite Myths and Legends*, p. 8, n. 3. Driver notes that Danel and Daniel have divergent spellings in Hebrew. Also M. Noth, 'Noah, Daniel und Hiob in Ezechiel XIV', *VT* 1 (1951), pp. 252–3.

[6] *Aqhat* II.v.8ff., *Canaanite Myths and Legends*, pp. 52–53.

[7] *Aqhat* II.v.3–7, *ibid.*, pp. 52–53.

[8] Baal mediates with El on his behalf (*Aqhat* II.i.21–34, *ibid.*, pp. 48–49) and Danel employs the name of Baal in his incantations (*Aqhat* I.iii.1ff., *ibid.*, pp. 62–63).

[9] *Aqhat* I.ii.35, *ibid.*, pp. 60–61.

Ugaritic myth a connection between Danel and a holy mountain. The extant *Aqhat*, however, bears no resemblance to a Paradise myth, and so I hesitate to improve on Herrmann's suggestion and to say that a comparison of the King of Tyre before his fall with the wise and righteous Danel is a factor in the prophet's handling of 28.11ff.

The commentators[1] may be right in supposing that there is an ironical intention in 28.3 ('Behold you are wiser than Danel'), but we miss the point of the prophet's use of the myth in vv. 11ff., if we assume that he is merely being ironical in ascribing wisdom and perfection to the King of Tyre. It is the *fall* of the King of Tyre as a consequence of his intoxication with wealth and power on which the prophet wishes to focus attention and this is why he uses the myth of his previous sojourn in Paradise on the mountain of God in a state of wisdom and integrity.

What he wishes to establish is that the present claim of the king to wisdom and power is the monstrous *hubris* of a fallen being who has been banished from Paradise and does not know the limits of his creatureliness. But then this would be true of all those who believed in the self-sufficiency of *'ēṣā* or *ḥoḵmā* and who supposed that, independent of God, they wielded the power to shape events. The vocabulary of wisdom is applicable to man in Paradise conscious of his creaturely limits and his dependence on God, but when it is used ebulliently in a context of humanism, whether of statecraft or of commercial operations, it is *hubris* and the usurping of God's role.

In 28.4–5 the *ḥoḵmā* and *tᵉḇūnā* of the King of Tyre are directly associated with his ability for organizing trade and amassing wealth. When he says 'I am God' or 'I am a god' (vv. 2, 9) this is not a cultic apotheosis—a laying claim to divine honours[2]—but the expression of an unbridled confidence in the impregnability of his island fortress and in his ability to mount gigantic commercial

[1] So H. A. Redpath, *The Book of the Prophet Ezekiel* (Westminster Commentaries, 1907), *in loc.* Also Herrmann, Bertholet and Cooke.

[2] *Pace* Redpath. Cooke says that 'I am a god' is hardly a boast of divine descent, but a blasphemous word of self-exaltation (similarly Bertholet). Herrmann understands 'I occupy the seat of God (or "the gods") in the heart of the seas' to refer to the impregnable island fortress of Tyre. Similarly Cooke, who, however, makes the alternative suggestion that the reference is to the empty throne of Melqarth in the temple at Tyre which the king presumed to claim.

enterprises and bring them inevitably to fruition. There are three phrases which deserve special attention in this connection:

Verse 2: 'And you have put your mind (*lēḇ*) on par with God's mind (*lēḇ*).'
Verse 6: 'Because you have put your mind (*lēḇ*) on par with God's mind (*lēḇ*).'
Verse 5: 'And your mind (*lēḇ*) has become arrogant because of your wealth.'
Cf. v. 2, 'Because your mind is arrogant' and v. 17, 'Your mind is arrogant'.

Verses 2 and 6 mean that the King of Tyre behaves as if he had the mental capacity (*lēḇ*) of God; as if he were in absolute control of events and could always bend them to his plans; as if with his foresight and acumen he had the world at his feet. Verse 5 traces this conviction to his intoxication with wealth and power (*ḥayil*) and to his conviction that there is no enterprise which he cannot plan and bring to success by his wisdom and perspicacity.

In the passage as a whole wealth is regarded as one of the principal ingredients of power.[1] The King of Tyre behaves as if his wealth harnessed to his commercial genius places him on a par with the power and mental grasp of God. But against this megalomaniac fantasy the prophet sets the realism of Yahweh's word. On the day when the Babylonians execute that word of judgment it will be seen that history is shaped by a spiritual power making for righteousness and that the King of Tyre, for all his economic resources, is man and not God (vv. 2, 9; cf. Isa. 31.3).

[1] Cf. 28.5: 'Through the wide scope of your wisdom in commercial operations you have amassed wealth (*ḥayil*) and you have become arrogant because of your wealth.' *Ḥayil* is 'power through wealth' or 'power through economic resources'. See W. McKane, 'The *Gibbôr Ḥayil* in the Israelite Community', *Transactions of the Glasgow University Oriental Society*, 17 (1959), pp. 31ff.

VI

WISDOM AND POWER BELONG TO YAHWEH ALONE

THE difference between the following passages and those in chapter V is that the positive aspect of the prophetic position appears more clearly in them, whereas the former group advances a negative polemic against the claims of old wisdom. There are, however, one or two passages in chapter V which might equally well have been discussed in this chapter (e.g. Isa. 10.13ff., 29.14–16).

Isaiah 14.24–27

Yahweh is a *yōʿēṣ* whose policy in relation to Egypt and Assyria is clearly formulated and will be effectively carried out. 'As I have deliberated (*dimmīṯī*, cf. 10.7) so it will come to pass and as I have planned so it will be implemented' (*tāqūm*).[1] He has planned (*yāʿaṣ*) to break the power of Assyria and to set his people free from her yoke, but this is only one facet of his *ʿēṣā*, which embraces the whole earth, and, in respect of this world-wide policy, his executive power matches his planning genius. 'This is the policy which Yahweh has made for all the earth and this is the hand which is stretched out (sc. to put the policy into effect) over all nations.' Yahweh is the only person entitled to call himself a *yōʿēṣ*, for when he makes a policy (*yāʿaṣ*) no one can abrogate it (*yāpēr*),[2] and when he acts to put his plan into effect, no one can enforce a stay of execution.

So in reality it is Yahweh who has the acumen and power which the professional statesmen imagine that they possess and by which they claim to shape the destiny of their own and other nations. The political sagacity in which they pride themselves is, after all, as

[1] Cf. Jer. 23.20 and Isa. 31.2 (*lōʾ hēsīr*). Also J. Fichtner, 'Jahves Plan in der Botschaft des Jesaja', p. 22, n. 25.

[2] Cf. Isa. 44.25; Ps. 33.10.

insubstantial as a bubble, for *ʿēṣā* in truth belongs to Yahweh and not to the nicely calculated more or less of diplomacy.[1]

Isaiah 19.1–3

These verses describe disunity and strife in Egypt at every level of corporate life, between individuals, municipalities and kingdoms. This breakdown of national solidarity and relapse into internecine warfare is attributed to Yahweh who has dissolved the acumen (*lēḇāḇ*) of Egypt, laid waste her morale or *esprit de corps* (*rūaḥ*) and devoured her political judgment (*ʿēṣā*). In default of the acumen on which the country normally relied for good government recourse is had to extraordinary measures and guidance is sought by means of necromancy, but Yahweh's policy for Egypt will be implemented and he will deliver[2] her into the hands of a hard master, destroying her economic prosperity at its source by drying up the Nile (vv. 4ff.). Cf. 19.12, 17. The mention of the land of Judah will strike fear into the hearts of the Egyptians because of the policy (*ʿēṣā*) of Yahweh of Hosts which he has formulated (*yāʿaṣ*) against Egypt.[3]

Isaiah 28.24–29

Yahweh is the source of agricultural science and the man who practises correct methods is disciplined (*ysr*) and instructed (*yrh*) by him. Yahweh has established a system (*mišpāṭ*) and a rule (*tōrā*) for agriculture, so that in this sphere also he is wonderful in *ʿēṣā* and great in *tūšīyā*. The meaning of *tūšīyā*[4] and its affinity with the vocabulary of wisdom can best be seen in the following passages:

(*a*) In Prov. 3.21, where it is coupled with the ethically neutral and sometimes pejorative *mᵉzimmā*. Also in Prov. 8.14, where it is coupled with *ʿēṣā* and these two are matched in the second half of

[1] Cf. J. Fichtner, *ibid.*, p. 24, who notes that the vocabulary of wisdom is being used in this passage, but who does not associate this with a prophetic riposte to the claims of wisdom.

[2] *skr* = *sgr* (?).

[3] Similarly Isa. 23.8–9 against Tyre. It is Yahweh's policy to bring her to judgment and to destroy and dishonour her.

[4] Cf. H. Bauer, *ZAW* 48 (1930), p. 77. To be derived from *yēš* < *yēšay*, with a primary meaning 'what is in existence', i.e. 'power', 'capacity', 'competence'.

the line by *bînā* and *g^e^bûrā*. Hence *'ēṣā* and *tûšîyā* is a collocation closely comparable to *'ēṣā* and *g^e^bûrā* in Isa. 36.5.[1]

(*b*) In Job 6.13 where it is parallel to *'ezrā*, 'help', and in Job 12.16 where it is coupled with *'ōz*, 'strength', both contexts pointing to the meaning 'power', 'capacity', 'competence'. It is clear that *tûšîyā* is another word which illustrates the practical bent of old wisdom and its close associations with the idea of effective and successful action.[2]

Isaiah 40.12–17

Who other than Yahweh has measured the capacity of the waters in the hollow of his hand and estimated[3] the heavens with the span of his hand? Who but Yahweh has collected for measurement in a *šālîs* (?) the dust of the earth or weighed the mountains on a balance and the hills on scales? That is to say, Yahweh can measure with supreme ease and so manage with the greatest precision the vastnesses of nature.

But his precise control and executive power are demonstrated with equal impressiveness in the field of history. What *yō'ēṣ* has ever given him advice? Whom did he ever consult (*nō'āṣ*) in order to have his thoughts clarified (*way^e^bînēhû*)? Who ever taught him what constitutes the right order of things (*mišpāṭ*) or who divulged to him the way of perspicacity (*t^e^bûnōṯ*)? Yahweh's control over history is effortless and consummate, for the nations are as a drop from a bucket and are reckoned by him as dust on the scales. All the nations are as nothing before him; he counts them as illusory and unreal.

Since Yahweh does not need the services of a *yō'ēṣ*, the claims of the *yō'ēṣ* and the *ḥākām* are seen to be hollow, especially when the mental capacity of Yahweh is properly appreciated. He alone has a *lēb* which commands admiration and *'ēṣā* and *t^e^bûnā* are properly

[1] See above, p. 67.

[2] Cf. H. Duesberg, *op. cit.*, i, pp. 251–2. *tûšîyā* means 'prudence allied to force'.

[3] Cf. G. R. Driver, 'Hebrew Notes on Prophetic Books', *VT* 1 (1951), pp. 242–3. Driver argues that 'estimated' is an unjustifiable translation of *tkn* and that its underlying sense, as an expanded form of *kûn*, is seen in Aramaic *takkēn* = Hebrew *hēkîn*, *kōnēn*, meaning 'adjusted (to standard)', 'set right'. In Driver's opinion this sense suits all the Old Testament occurrences and the meaning 'measured' has crept in as appearing to suit the context of a few passages. Isa. 40.12 is certainly such a passage, for the *parallelismus membrorum* indicates that *tikkēn* is more or less synonymous with *māḏaḏ* and supports the translation 'estimated'.

attributable only to him. That statesmen should describe their role by means of the vocabulary of wisdom is evidence only of a vast conceit, for *ʿēṣā* and *tᵉḇūnā* belong to Yahweh and it is he who has the mental grasp and the power to shape history to his own ends.

Isaiah 40.28–31

Yahweh, the creator of the ends of the earth, is not subject to human limitations and fatigue and there is no possibility of conducting research into his perspicacity (*tᵉḇūnā*). His strength is of a different kind and a higher order than the physical strength of men in the prime of life and he bestows this on those who are jaded and strengthless. Hence when those at the peak of physical condition are worn out and stumble with fatigue, those who wait on Yahweh will exchange weakness for strength, they will soar on the wing like eagles, they will run and not be exhausted, they will walk and not be fatigued. This should be regarded as a metaphorical description of a spiritual strength (*kōaḥ*) and not as an assertion that those who wait on Yahweh will outlast the physical vigour of young men in their prime.

Isa. 30.15–16 is a passage similarly conceived. There the prophet says that salvation or liberty (*yᵉšūʿā*) resides in penitence (*šūḇā*) and a serene, trustful confidence in Yahweh. This posture is the source of a superior kind of strength (*gᵉḇūrā*), but the people prefer to put their reliance on horses. Akin to this is the contrast which is drawn between spirit (*rūaḥ*) and flesh (*bāśār*) in Isa. 31.3, and again in 7.4, where Isaiah urges an attitude of calm trustfulness on Ahaz when he is threatened by the Syrian-Ephraimite coalition; Ahaz, however, prefers *bāśār* to *rūaḥ* and looks for security in a pact with Assyria.[1]

Isaiah 46.10–11

Only Yahweh can predict the shape of the future, because he is never lacking in the power which is required to implement his policies and so events are always responsive to his plan. Hence he says: 'My policy (*ʿēṣā*) will be implemented[2] and I shall do whatever

[1] Cf. Jer. 10.12; 51.15. Yahweh made the earth by his power (*kōaḥ*), founded the world by his wisdom and stretched out the heavens by his perspicacity (*tᵉḇūnā*). 'Perspicacity' here is architectonic flair or grasp.

[2] See above, p. 79.

I will to do.' In particular Cyrus, the bird of prey whom he summons from the distant east, is a man of Yahweh's *'ēṣā*[1] who is to exercise a decisive influence on history. Referring to what he will effect through Cyrus, Yahweh says: 'What I have spoken I will bring to pass; what I have shaped I will execute.' The *dāḇār* of Yahweh concerning Cyrus will be fulfilled, for Cyrus is a man of Yahweh's *'ēṣā* who will implement his policy.

Jeremiah 9.11–12 [12–13]

The prophet is speaking about the ruin of Jerusalem and Judah and is asking why the land should be burned up like a desert and abandoned. Who among the statesmen (*ḥᵃḵāmīm*) of Judah has real insight into the meaning of her ruin? Or who among those who claim to be Yahweh's prophets has ever essayed such an explanation? ('To whom has the mouth of Yahweh spoken that he should divulge it?') As the bearer of Yahweh's *dāḇār*, Jeremiah answers the question about the reason for Jerusalem's ruin. 'Because they have forgotten my instruction (*tōrā*) which I set before them and do not pay attention to my voice nor proceed in accordance with it.' The passage is directed against two classes of opponents, the false prophets (like Hananiah, ch. 28) who are out of touch with reality and prophesy security, while the nation stands on the edge of disaster, and the statesmen of Judah who pride themselves in their political skill and perspicacity but under whose direction the country lurches blindly to disaster. The only reliable political commentator is the prophet, since he is the bearer of the *dāḇār* by which Yahweh's *'ēṣā* is communicated.

Jeremiah 19.7–15

Yahweh will lay waste the *'ēṣā* of Judah and Jerusalem, i.e. the policies of her statesmen devised for her security will prove worthless because they contradict Yahweh's *'ēṣā*. Jerusalem will be besieged and reduced to famine conditions and will fall in a day of disaster and carnage, when her inhabitants will be given to the sword before her enemies. This end is coming to Jerusalem because she has refused to hear Yahweh's words (15). The prophet who communicates Yahweh's *'ēṣā* and so is the only authentic source of

[1] Following the Qᵉrē: *'īš 'ᵃṣāṯī*.

political guidance has been ignored and spurned, but vindication is at hand and the prophetic *dāḇār* will be fulfilled in judgment.

Jeremiah 23.20

The wrath of Yahweh will not turn back until he has executed (*ʿaśōṯō*) and implemented (*haqīmō*)[1] what he has planned (*mezimmōṯ libbō*). At the end of days you will reflect on it with clear understanding (*tiṯbōnenū ḇāh bīnā*). *Bīnā* is used here of the transparency of insight which is produced by the carrying out of Yahweh's judgment 'at the end of days', when his policy for the world is fully implemented. We have already remarked that *mezimmā* is an ethically neutral word which can be used pejoratively,[2] but here it refers to Yahweh's capacity to devise a policy which can be effectively carried out (cf. Jer. 30.24). The same point is made by Jer. 32.19, which states that Yahweh of Hosts is great in *ʿēṣā* and mighty in action (*hāʿalīlīyā*).[3] The purpose of *ʿēṣā* is to achieve results—it reaches completion in action.[4] Thus the context (vv. 20–23) deals with Yahweh's effective interventions in the history of Israel in salvation and judgment and so it is Yahweh (and not the statesmen) who plans and directs Israel's life, and the prophet, contrary to what the *śārīm* represent, is a key political figure.

Jeremiah 49.20

Here the prophet pronounces judgment against Edom: 'Therefore hear the policy (*ʿēṣā*) of Yahweh which he has made (*yāʿaṣ*) against Edom and the plans (*maḥašāḇōṯ*) which he has worked out (*ḥāšaḇ*) against the inhabitants of Teman' (exactly parallel is 50.45 against Babylon).

Obadiah vv. 8ff.

Yahweh will wipe out *ḥaḵāmīm* from Edom and perspicacity (*teḇūnā*) from the mount of Esau 'on that day' (cf. Jer. 23.20, 'at the end of days'). Edom had a reputation for wisdom,[5] but however

[1] See above, pp. 79, 82.
[2] See above, p. 80. For the pejorative use of *mezimmā* see Jer. 11.15; Pss. 10.2, 4; 21.12 [11]; 37.7; 139.20; Prov. 12.2; 24.8; Job 21.27. Cf. H. Duesberg, *op. cit.*, i, p. 252.
[3] Perhaps the reading should be *hāʿalīlā*.
[4] See above, pp. 66ff.
[5] Cf. I Kings 5.9 [4.29]ff. See above, p. 73.

skilful and shrewd her political advisers it will avail her nothing in the day when Yahweh's judgment falls on her. Edom gloated over the fall of Jerusalem (v. 12) and exploited Judah's disaster for her own gain (v. 13) and this is the sin for which she will be punished. It is morality which moves the world and not political shrewdness. This is the *'ēṣā* of Yahweh which will be implemented against Edom.

Psalm 33.6–11

The heavens were made by the word (*dāḇār*) of Yahweh and all the heavenly bodies by the breath (*rūaḥ*) of his mouth (v. 6). In creating the world he spoke and it came to pass, he gave the command and it was implemented[1] (v. 9). This locating of Yahweh's creative power in his *dāḇār* and *rūaḥ* points to its otherness from the power which is located in *bāśār*.[2] It is of a superior quality to this crude power; it is a refined spiritual power. Yahweh annuls (*hēpīr*) the *'ēṣā* of the nations and thwarts (or 'vetoes') the political calculations (*maḥšāḇōṯ*) of the peoples.[3] The *'ēṣā* of Yahweh is always implemented (*ta'amōḏ*), the calculations of his mind (*lēḇ*) are for all generations (vv. 10–11).[4]

[1] *wayya'amōḏ*.

[2] Cf. Isa. 7.4; 30.15–16; 31.3. In 11.4 'the rod (or "sceptre") of his mouth'= *dāḇār*.

[3] Translating the perfects *hēpīr* and *hēnī'* as frequentatives.

[4] I include this, although it is not prophetical, because of its affinity, in respect of the use made of the vocabulary of wisdom, with the other passages in this chapter.

VII

THE PROPHETIC REINTERPRETATION OF THE VOCABULARY OF WISDOM

Hosea 4.6

ISRAEL is reduced to silence—the silence of ignorance, perplexity and discomfiture—for lack of knowledge (*da'aṯ*), and responsibility falls on the priest who has rejected knowledge and forgotten the instruction (*tōrā*) of God. *Da'aṯ* is the instruction which the priest ought to have imparted to the people and it is for want of this priestly instruction that they are dumb. *Da'aṯ*, then, is used along with *tōrā* of a corpus of traditional material, comprising a recitation of the mighty acts done by Yahweh for Israel—an account of Israel's distinctive understanding of her historical existence under Yahweh—and also a statement of what was required of her in the way of response to Yahweh's demands.[1] Cf. Isa. 28.9, where the knowledge (*da'aṯ*) in which the prophet instructs (*yōre*) the people and the tradition (*š^emū'ā*) which he expounds (*yāḇīn*) are brushed aside by his opponents as juvenile.

Hosea 14.10 [9][2]

The man who is wise (*ḥāḵām*) and perspicacious (*nāḇōn*) is he who discerns (*hēḇīn*) and knows Yahweh's ways. For Yahweh's ways are straight (*y^ešārīm*), i.e. consistently good and just, and the righteous walk in them, but those who defy Yahweh's demands (*pōš^e'īm*) stumble in them.

This means that Yahweh imposes a plan and an order on historical existence (his *'ēṣā*) and that the wise and far-seeing man

[1] Cf. J. L. McKenzie, 'Knowledge of God in Hosea', *JBL* 74 (1955), pp. 22–27. I am not convinced by McKenzie's attempt to show that the meaning of *da'aṯ* in Hosea is to be limited to traditional Hebrew morality or by his associated argument that 'knowledge of Elohim' means less than 'knowledge of Yahweh'.

[2] I am not really concerned to raise critical questions here. It does not matter for this study whether or not this is a later addition to the book of Hosea. J. Lindblom, *Prophecy in Ancient Israel*, p. 392, thinks 14.6 [5]ff. is an exilic addition, while A. Bentzen, *Introduction* ii, p. 133, remarks that there is nothing in 14.2 [1]ff. which is indicative of post-exilic origin. See below on Ps. 32.8.

is he who lives in harmony with this order and responds obediently to its moral demands. Where the actions of men are opposed to Yahweh's demands, they will come into conflict with his policy and be exposed to his judgment, for he never fails to give effect to his plans.

The wise and perspicacious man is no longer (as in the context of old wisdom) he who has cured himself of sloppy thinking and rash speaking through a rigorous mental discipline, and has become a hard thinker and a clear speaker. The assumption which underlies this use of *ḥāḵām* and *nāḇōn* is not that human reason is self-sufficient in the sphere of statesmanship. The words do not refer to native sagacity, intellectual equipment, penetrating thought, nicety of judgment. They do not belong any more to a critical uncommitted method of enquiry, but are yoked to the assumptions of a religious faith and to a moralism which derives from it.[1] The same can be said of Hos. 4.14, where the people's lack of *bînā* or *t*ᵉ*ḇûnā* (*'ām lō' yāḇîn*) consists in harlotry, adultery and cult prostitution. Also Isa. 1.3: 'Israel does not know, my people do not reflect (*lō' hiṯbōnān*)', where it is Israel's obtuseness and rebelliousness in relation to Yahweh's ways which are in question. Likewise in Isa. 43.10 *tēḏ*ᵉ*'ū, ta'*ᵃ*mînū* and *tāḇînū* are used of a discerning knowledge of Yahweh and a steadfast belief in him who alone is God. To acquire this insight and firm belief one must be committed as a witness and a servant.

Micah 4.11–12[2]

Many nations are poised to strike against Jerusalem, to pollute her sanctuary and to gaze on her with vulgar curiosity, but their plans will come to nothing because they conflict with Yahweh's policy. Such nations are ignorant of the political calculations (*maḥšāḇōṯ*) of Yahweh and have no insight (*lō' hēḇînū*) into his policy (*'ēṣā*). They suppose that they are poised to take Jerusalem,

[1] Cf. H. Duesberg, *op. cit.*, i, pp. 260–9. Duesberg notes that such vocabulary as *ṣeḏeq, mišpāṭ, yōšer* and *tōm* involves ethical assumptions.

[2] See my remark on p. 86, n. 2. J. Lindblom, *Prophecy in Ancient Israel*, p. 251, n. 60, holds that Micah 4.11–13 refers to the siege of Jerusalem in 701 BC. It does not come from Micah, but is to be attributed to a nationalistic prophet who was perhaps closely associated with the Jerusalem temple and who was a prophet of national weal. Also *Micha literarisch untersucht* (1929), pp. 9ff. Cf. A. Bentzen, *Introduction*, ii, p. 148, who attributes most of the material in Micah 4–5 to an anti-Assyrian, nationalistic milieu which has connections with the circle of Isaiah's disciples.

but in fact they are assembled to receive Yahweh's judgment—he has gathered them as sheaves to the threshing-floor. They do not know Yahweh in the prophetic sense of 'know'.[1] That is, they are unaware that Yahweh is active within history submitting nations to an ethical scrutiny and exposing to judgment those who do not pass his test. *Hēḇînû* has also been brought into subjection to the prophetic faith and 'insight' or 'perspicacity' is not now a native mental capacity educed by intellectual discipline and experience, but a view of the political scene from the standpoint of faith in Yahweh as the only effective policy-maker and executive.

Jeremiah 3.15

The 'shepherds' are those who direct the affairs of Judah and are charged with her security; *śeḵel* ('aptitude') and *lēḇ* ('mind' or 'mental grasp') are two of the intellectual virtues of the professional statesman, developed by educational discipline and indicative of his open, critical approach to politics. Here it is implied that Yahweh alone can give effective political guidance (shepherding) to his community and that vocabulary of this kind can only be properly used of his planning and surveillance. It is Yahweh's mental grasp which is creative of the true *ʿēṣā* and when rulers (shepherds) of the community have access to this (as they can have through the *dāḇār* of a prophet) they direct affairs with knowledge (*dēʿā*) and aptitude (*haśkēl*), and then the nation will no longer be rebellious, disobedient and idolatrous (v. 13). 'Knowledge' and 'aptitude' are now equated with religious illumination and obedience and are not the intellectual virtues of a self-contained humanist system of political sagacity.

Jeremiah 4.22

Judah is foolish (*'ᵉwîl*) and her people do not know Yahweh. They are foolish (*sᵉḵālîm*) children and are not far-seeing (*nᵉḇōnîm*); they are wise (*ḥᵃḵāmîm*) to do evil, but they do not know how to do good. The folly of Judah and her lack of perspicacity consist in her not knowing Yahweh or in her not knowing how to do good. The latter phrase expresses summarily the prophetic understanding of 'knowledge of Yahweh' which is an expression of high ethical

[1] See below on Jer. 4.22.

earnestness.[1] That is to say, knowing Yahweh implies outright ethical commitment (cf. especially Jer. 22.15–16: 'Did not your father eat and drink and do justice and righteousness? Then it was well with him. He meted out justice to the poor and needy. Is not this to know me? says Yahweh.')

'They are wise to do evil', on the other hand, may refer to the indifference of old wisdom to such passionate ethical commitment. The *ḥāḵām* was the man who could devise a policy which was intellectually coherent and was an effective means of reaching a desiderated goal, and it was by this and not any ethical criterion that the 'wisdom' of such a policy was judged.

Jeremiah 9.22–23

The *ḥāḵām* is not to glory in his *ḥoḵmā* nor the strong man (*gibbōr*) in his strength nor the rich man in his wealth. Whoever would boast, let him boast in this, that he grasps (*haśkēl*) and knows (*yāḏōaʿ*) Yahweh, for it is he who does *ḥeseḏ, mišpāṭ* and *ṣᵉḏāqā* on the earth. Here, as in Hos. 4.6 and Isa. 28.9, 'knowledge of Yahweh' is a knowledge of the *Heilsgeschichte*, an awareness of Yahweh's methods of imposing his will on historical existence and creating a political and social order which conforms to his moral demands.[2] It is not my intention to embark on a detailed discussion of *ḥeseḏ, mišpāṭ* and *ṣᵉḏāqā*, but they certainly mean that, in the ordering of civilized life, Yahweh will enforce his steadfast moral purpose and this is all I am concerned to establish here. Because Yahweh acts with loyalty, justice and righteousness, nations are tested for survival and are judged according to their ethical fitness.

To grasp and to know Yahweh is to be conscious of the constancy of his moral purpose which sustains his actions in the shaping of history and to know why one nation stands and another falls. This is a knowledge to which traditional priestly instruction (*tōrā*), with its recitation of God's mighty acts and its statement of

[1] Cf. J. Lindblom, *Prophecy in Ancient Israel*, pp. 310–11, 340–1. See below on Jer. 9.22–23.

[2] J. Lindblom, 'Wisdom in the Old Testament Prophets', p. 199, seems to deny that 'knowledge of Yahweh' is a prophetic counterblast to the claims of wisdom in those passages where it is associated with *ḥoḵmā, bīnā, tᵉḇūnā*, etc. I am not certain, however, that this is what he is saying. If he means no more than that the prophetic concept of 'knowledge of Yahweh' is not derived from wisdom teaching, his statement is unobjectionable.

his demands, contributes, and it is also communicated by the prophetic *dāḇār*, whether it be a demand for repentance or a threat of judgment against those who have not kept loyalty with Yahweh nor done justice and righteousness. In either case it is directed against those who have not responded to Yahweh's requirements so as to live in harmony with the pattern of his activity within history and with the social order which he supports.[1]

The person who has this knowledge of Yahweh is truly a *ḥāḵām*, but the old-fashioned *ḥāḵām* who confidently relies on his self-contained political sagacity has no insight into reality and neither the strong man[2] nor the rich man[3] has the power to shape events with which he credits himself.

Jeremiah 10.21

The 'shepherds' (i.e. those responsible for the safety and welfare of the community; cf. Jer. 3.15) are brutish; they have not sought access to Yahweh's policy (*'ēṣā*). Consequently they have no grasp (*lō' hiśkîlû*) of the situation and all the flock is scattered. *drš* ('sought access') may refer to a recourse to the oracle for guidance or to the prophetic *dāḇār*, but, in either case, the attitude to old wisdom is significantly different from that which underlies the story of Ahithophel.[4] It is now asserted that statesmen cannot have a grasp of affairs unless they have access to Yahweh's policy (*'ēṣā*).

The implication of this is that credence is no longer given as in the Ahithophel story to the concept of two alternative systems of guidance, each of equal validity, the one deriving from a humanist aptitude (*śeḵel*) and the other from a revealed word. *Śeḵel* which, in the context of old wisdom, is achieved through a rigorous intellectual discipline and a mastery of the techniques of statecraft cannot now be attained (so our passage implies) except through access to Yahweh's policy.

With this should be compared Ps. 14.2 (53.3 [2]). Yahweh looks down from heaven to see if there is anyone who is *maśkîl*, who seeks guidance (*dōrēš*) from God. The moralism which is charac-

[1] N. W. Porteous, 'Old Testament Theological Thought-Forms', *SJT* (1954), is to be followed in his assertion that 'knowledge of Yahweh' includes the human response to Yahweh's mighty acts and is not just the proclamation of these mighty acts.

[2] See above, pp. 72–3ff. on Isa. 31.1–3, and 85 on Ps. 33.6–11.

[3] See above, pp. 73ff. on Ezek. 28.3ff.

[4] See above, pp. 55ff.

teristic of this reinterpretation of the vocabulary of wisdom[1] is perhaps to be seen in Ps. 41.2 [1]: 'Blessed is he who is *maśkīl* towards the weak', i.e. who has insight into their need and fulfils Yahweh's demand for compassion by giving them effective aid.[2]

Jeremiah 23.5

Yahweh will raise up for David a righteous branch and he will reign as king and act with a grasp of affairs (*wᵉhiśkīl*). The connection between *śkl* and practical competence is retained, but a context of ethical commitment is presupposed. The man who has *śeḵel* is he who does *mišpāṭ* and *ṣᵉḏāqā*.

To conclude this chapter I append a number of passages not from prophetic books but illustrating a usage of the vocabulary of wisdom similar to that of the passages just reviewed.

Deuteronomy 32.28–29

This passage deals with Israel's lack of insight into Yahweh's mighty acts of salvation and judgment. It is said of Israel that she is a nation devoid of policies (*'ēṣōṯ*) and without perspicacity (*tᵉḇūnā*). If her people were wise they would grasp (*yaśkīlū*) the pattern of Yahweh's activity in history and would discern (*yāḇīnū*) their latter end. Similarly Deut. 32.6, where, in respect of failures of awareness and response in relation to Yahweh's mighty works, Israel is described as a people *nāḇāl* and not *ḥāḵām*. To be compared with this is Ps. 106.7: 'Our fathers in Egypt did not grasp (*lō' hiśkīlū*) the wonderful acts of Yahweh.' This means that they had no understanding of the meaning of his activity within history; they did not grasp the pattern of his interventions and so they did not remember the numerous evidences of his loyalty (*rōḇ ḥᵃsāḏeḵā*). Hence they rebelled against him at the Red Sea. *Śeḵel* is here a religious insight into the mighty acts by which Yahweh shapes history so as to lead his people in accordance with his *'ēṣā*.

Psalm 32.8

'I will give you [sing.] aptitude (*'aśkīlᵉḵā*) and will instruct you (*'ōrᵉḵā*) in the way in which you should go. I will give you advice,

[1] Cf. Jer. 4.22; 9.22–23; 22.15–16.

[2] Cf., however, *BH*, according to which *maśkîl* is the title of the psalm. Verse 2 is then read with G. and T.: 'Blessed is the poor and needy man, in an evil day Yahweh will deliver him.'

my son.'[1] Perhaps we should regard this as a psalm which contains a blend of wisdom and Israelite legal piety. I have included this passage and Hos. 14.10 [9] in this chapter, because they do exhibit a usage of the vocabulary of wisdom similar to that of the other passages. They differ from them, however, in one important respect. Whereas the prophets characteristically address themselves to the nation it is the individual who is addressed in these two passages.

The psalmist in 32.8ff. gives his advice in a form reminiscent of the wisdom teacher. 'My son' (emended) recalls a stylistic feature of the 'Instruction' *Gattung*,[2] as do the imperatives in vv. 9 and 11, while the vocabulary is recognizably that of wisdom (*śkl, yrh, yʿṣ* and *bīn*). Moreover the teaching still has its connection with the personal experience of the teacher, although its content no longer rests exclusively on his authority as the acknowledged master of a tried and tested educational discipline. The teaching now rests particularly on his religious experience and it points beyond himself to Yahweh. The way in which the instructed must go is a way of contrition (vv. 1–2, 5); the grasp (*śeḵel*), instruction (*tōrā*) and advice (*ʿēṣā*) which the teacher imparts are creative of trust in Yahweh and the loyalty (*ḥeseḏ*) which derives from trust. The lot of the wicked man (*rāšāʿ*) is contrasted with that of the trustful (*habbōṭēaḥ* YHWH) and the righteous (*ṣaddīq, yešar lēḇ*).

We see here the transformation of the vocabulary of wisdom under the impact of religious faith and practice, with their clean-cut ethical distinctions and passionate commitment to righteousness. This reinterpretation should probably be traced to Israelite legal piety, as the preoccupation with the individual would suggest, but with its demand for contrition, trust and righteousness it shows a marked similarity to the prophetic use of the vocabulary of wisdom.

Psalm 36.4 [3]

'The words of his mouth are evil and deceit (*'āwen ūmirmā*). He has no longer a grasp of virtue (*ḥāḏal lehaśkīl lehēṭīḇ*)'. Thus aptitude or grasp is envisaged in a particular connection with virtue.

[1] Reading *benī* with *BH*. MT, *ʿēnī*: 'I will counsel you with my eye upon you.' So RSV.

[2] See above, p. 44.

Ps. 101.2 is a similar case: 'I shall grasp (*'aśkīlā*) a way of integrity' (literally: 'I shall have insight in a perfect way'). The context (vv. 2–4) shows that this 'grasp' is associated with the avoidance of evil and the doing of good. The psalmist sings of *ḥeseḏ* and *mišpāṭ* (v. 1) and describes himself as a man of integrity (*'eṯhallēḵ b^eṯom l^eḇāḇī*) whom he contrasts with the man lacking in integrity (*lēḇāḇ 'iqqēš*, 'a twisted mind').

VIII

WISDOM AS ESOTERIC KNOWLEDGE

ISAIAH 47.9–13[1] is a polemic against Babylon in connection with the long training involved in acquiring the specialist skills of spells (*ḥaḇārīm*)[2] and incantations (*kešāpīm*). Babylon is wearied through having too many sources of advice (*ʿēṣōṯ*). Let the astrologers and star-gazers who predict the future at the new moon[3] save her if they can (v. 13). Babylon has been led astray by her wisdom and knowledge, but, in spite of her many incantations and the great power of her spells, she is ripe for Yahweh's judgment and disaster will overtake her.

Similarly 44.25–26 which is directed against the 'wise' and particularly against those who claim to be able to predict the future through their mastery of specialized occult techniques. Yahweh, who created the heavens and the earth, alone knows what the future holds, and so he annuls (*mēp̄ēr*) the omens of seer-priests (reading *bārīm*, Akkadian *bārū*)[4] and makes fools of diviners. He turns the sages (*ḥaḵāmīm*) backwards and makes their knowledge idiotic. With this spurious esoteric knowledge is contrasted the *dāḇār* of the servant (*ʿeḇeḏ*) or messenger (*mal'āḵ*)[5] of Yahweh by which Yahweh's *ʿēṣā* is communicated. This is a policy which will certainly be implemented and shape the future.

These passages reflect accurately the importance which was attached to the advice and activities of such masters of the occult for the purpose of securing the political future of Babylon. This is true both of the techniques for predicting the future (astrology, interpretation of dreams, inspection of omens, etc.) and of those

[1] Cf. A. Bentzen, *Introduction*, i, pp. 172–3.

[2] Cf. S. R. Driver, *Deuteronomy*[3] (ICC, 1902), p. 225. *ḥōḇēr ḥāḇer* is one who ties magic knots, who binds by a spell, who composes spells. L. Köhler, *Lexicon*, *s.v.* *ḥbr*.[2]

[3] Reading *'ašer* for *mē'ašer* (dittography of *m*) with G. and S.

[4] *bārīm* should also be read in Jer. 50.36. On the office of *bārū* see B. Meissner, *op. cit.*, ii, pp. 65–66, 242ff.

[5] Note that in Isa. 44.26 *mal'āḵ* is used of a prophet in association with *dāḇār* and *ʿēṣā*. See above, pp. 58ff.

for shaping the future (incantations, spells). The specialists in the various secret lores of prediction were politically influential and near the centre of government, since their advice was thought to be indispensable for the formulation of policy and the taking of right political decisions.[1] They held the keys to accurate forecasting and to the clarification of enigmatic phenomena thought to be pregnant with political significance, such as dreams or the movements of the heavenly bodies. Thus Thompson remarks: 'The soothsayer was as much a politician as the statesman and he was not slow in using the indications of political change to point the moral of his astrological observations.'[2]

The astrologers in particular were organized as an important department of political intelligence and sent in regular reports to the central government.[3] In view of all this I think that Eissfeldt[4] makes too sharp a distinction between 'scholars' and 'officials' in the Babylonian context and that the exegesis of Dan. 2.48–49 on which he so largely relies is questionable. Here he parts company with Montgomery and Bentzen, although the words in 2.49, 'but Daniel remained at the king's court', seem to me to point to the correctness of Montgomery's remark that Daniel was in the cabinet, while his friends were subordinate officials in their several provinces. I would judge also that it is unwise to conclude from the circumstance that Dan. 3 mentions only the conflict of Shadrach, Meshach and Abednego with other Babylonian political officials that Daniel is represented as a scholar presiding over a royal academy and not as a statesman. And are the specialists mentioned in chapter 2 really remote from political life? Does Eissfeldt suppose that the dream-interpreters and astrologers were really remote from political life? In fact, they were key political figures and the dividing line between scholars and statesmen in the context of the Babylonian higher civil service cannot be so easily drawn.

The important place occupied by the diviner and the magician

[1] Cf. Jer. 50.35–36, where the prophet threatens the Chaldaeans with the judgment of the sword and lists influential classes in the civil and military establishment (*śārīm, ḥakāmīm, bārīm* and *gibbōrīm*). Cf. Dan. 2.48–49; 3.30; 5.29ff.

[2] R. C. Thompson, *The Reports of the Magicians and Astrologers of Nineveh and Babylon* i–ii (1900), p. xv.

[3] R. C. Thompson, *ibid.*, p. xvi.

[4] O. Eissfeldt, 'Daniels und seiner drei Gefahrten Laufbahn im babylonischen, medischen und persischen Dienst', *ZAW* 62 (1960), pp. 246–57.

(the master of the word of power or efficacious ritual)[1] within the Judaean establishment is illustrated by Isa. 3.2–3 where the diviner (*qōsēm*), the skilful magician (*ḥᵃkam ḥᵃrāšîm*)[2] and the one who is knowledgeable in *laḥaš*[3] are classed with important military, civil and religious personages.

It is clear that this is a tradition of international wisdom altogether different in kind from the old wisdom which we have tried to define in the earlier part of this work. Old wisdom inculcated a critical, open mental posture; it discouraged doctrinaire assumptions; it was a pragmatic art of statesmanship which required that every case should be treated on its merits and that nothing should be attended to in drawing conclusions except the available evidence.

Here we have another type of wisdom which is also closely connected with the sphere of statecraft and political decisions, but which rests on a concept of esoteric knowledge or secret lore. The *ḥāḵām* is he who belongs to a closed corporation and who has acquired and mastered the secret techniques on which the art of prediction depends. Sometimes, as in the case of dreams, the phenomena which require to be interpreted are in themselves dark, opaque, enigmatic and lie unintelligible awaiting the special access which the *gnosis* of the seer-priest has to their riddle-like properties. The strong influence of this concept of wisdom in Babylonia is reflected in the very close connections between sage and priest and between wisdom and priestly lore.[4] That wisdom in this guise was

[1] Cf. the passages in the book of Exodus which deal with the efforts of the Egyptian magicians to match Aaron's rod with their 'secret arts'. Pharaoh (7.11) summoned his sages, sorcerers and magicians (perhaps *ḥᵃḵāmîm* is used here as a general term and what follows specifies the particular class of *ḥāḵām*; cf. *ḥᵃḵāmîm* in Isa. 44.25, specified by *bārîm* and *qōsᵉmîm*), and up to a point these specialists in magic are able to match Aaron's accomplishment with his rod, 'but Aaron's rod swallowed up their rods' (7.12). While the experts rely on their expertise (*bᵉlāṭêhem*), the power in Aaron's rod derives immediately from Yahweh (7.10). Ultimately the Egyptian specialists in magic are decisively defeated in this trial of strength with Yahweh (8.14 [18]) and admit that they are not the equal of the finger of God (8.15 [19]). Thus, even in this department of wisdom, the specialists are no match for Yahweh and are themselves the victims of the last plague (9.11).

[2] Perhaps *ḥᵃrāšîm* is a gloss *ex ḥᵃḏāšîm* ('new moons', 'new months') and we should read *ḥāḵām*, 'sage'. So *BH* and L. Köhler, *Lexicon*.

[3] *laḥaš* meaning 'whispering' perhaps refers to serpent-charming, i.e. to the procuring of an oracle from the 'whispering' of a snake. Cf. S. R. Driver, *op. cit.*, on Deut. 18.11. Driver points to *mᵉlaḥᵃšîm*, 'whisperers', 'snake-charmers', which is parallel to *ḥōḇēr ḥᵃḇārîm mᵉḥukkām* in Ps. 58.6 [5].

[4] Cf. L. Dürr, 'Das Erziehungswesen im Alten Testament und im Antiken Orient', p. 60. Dürr observes that the wise in Sumer and Akkad were properly the priests,

also influential in Judah is shown by Isa. 3.2–3, which has been discussed above.

The prophetic attitude to the claims of this wisdom is clearly formulated in the passages just reviewed. The power of such *ḥᵃḵāmīm* to predict or shape the future by their secret arts is denied. It is Yahweh alone who knows what the future holds and he communicates his policy through the word of his prophet (Isa. 44.25–26, 47.9–13). Nor is there any hint of the esoteric in the *dāḇār* of the prophet. It is a plain, open communication of Yahweh's *ʿēṣā* and anyone who has a mind to understand it has no need of an interpreter.

It is just in this respect that the response of Jewish apocalyptic to this brand of international wisdom is so much more complex and difficult to analyse. A full treatment of this would transgress the limits of this study, but the point can be well illustrated in connection with the book of Daniel, which, in agreement with Lindblom,[1] I should describe as the only book in the Old Testament which is fully-fledged apocalyptic, and in which we can examine the usage of the same vocabulary of wisdom as is employed by the prophets.

Daniel, along with other Jewish youths of royal and aristocratic families, is chosen to be educated for the higher civil service in Babylon. In this process of selection regard is had to physical soundness and to an impressive presence as well as to the intellectual stature of the candidates. To be of the right calibre to 'stand' in the royal palace (i.e. to be functionaries of the king) they require not only sharpness of intellect but an all-round physical and mental toughness (*kōaḥ*). These youths are selected for an arduous educational discipline—they are to be taught Babylonian language and letters[2] (Dan. 1.3–4).

Yet it is asserted that the acumen of four of those selected does not derive from this formal education (v. 5); God gave them

particularly the exorcist priests. On the common ideogram for priest and sage in Babylonia, see G. R. Driver, *Semitic Writing*, p. 62, n. 4. Cf. B. Meissner, *op. cit.*, ii, pp. 242–3. Meissner observes that the secret techniques of prediction were like magic regarded as pure science. 'This was not a secular activity; it was a mystery (*niṣirtu, piristu*) and the prerogative of a closed corporation of priests, especially the *bārū* priests.'

[1] J. Lindblom, *Prophecy in Ancient Israel*, p. 422.

[2] Cf. G. R. Driver, *Semitic Writing*, p. 65, who observes that the educational process took much longer than the three years mentioned in Dan. 1.5.

knowledge (*maddāʿ*) and grasp (*haśkēl*) in all letters and wisdom. Of Daniel in particular it is said that God endowed him with penetrative insight (*hēḇîn*) into visions and dreams (v. 17). Thus Daniel says of God in 2.22: 'He lays bare what is deep and concealed. He knows what is in the darkness and the light dwells with him.' Hence Daniel's faculty for clarifying dark and enigmatic dreams is to be traced not to his mastery of Babylonian techniques of prediction but to his endowment from God. It is this charismatic endowment which explains why Daniel succeeds where the Babylonian specialists in dream interpretation fail.

It should be noted, however, that the demand which Nebuchudrezzar makes upon the skill of his specialists is extraordinary and, in their opinion, unreasonable. His dream has left him in a state of deep, inner discomposure and he cannot recall its contents. So he asks his experts not only for the interpretation but for the recovery of the dream itself. Their normal function was to interpret dreams and so they reply: 'Let the king tell his servants the dream and we shall divulge its interpretation' (2.7, cf. 2.4). They protest that only the gods can pierce such a profound enigma (2.11) and so the stage is set for Daniel who, in every matter of wisdom and insight (*ḥoḵmā uḇînā*), is ten times better than the professionals (1.20, cf. 4.5), and to whom the God of heaven reveals the mystery in a vision of the night (2.19).

Daniel informs the king that the Babylonian sages who are experts in clarifying the enigmatic and illumining the future cannot confer intelligibility on this mystery, but that the God of heaven who lays bare mysteries has divulged it to him. Hence his unique luminosity of insight is not to be attributed to his technical excellence in the arts of clarification and prediction (2.27–30).[1]

The attitude of the Babylonian sages shows that it was the expected thing that a dream should be dark and opaque and should stand in need of interpretation (*pᵉšar*).[2] It was in supplying this that

[1] Cf. 2.45, 47; 4.6, 15 [9, 18].

[2] Cf. Gen. 41.8ff. The Egyptian experts are summoned by Pharaoh in order to interpret his dream, but no interpreter is forthcoming. *ptr* is cognate with Aramaic *pšr* (cf. *Hebrew pšr*, which according to Köhler is an Aramaic loan word; see *Lexicon*, *s.v.*). Cf. Akkadian *pāšir šunāti*, 'interpreter of dreams'. When Joseph is summoned to interpret the dream he disclaims all personal credit for his skill and asserts that it is God who is the interpreter of dreams (vv. 15–16). Joseph therefore pierces the opaqueness of the dream phenomena not through the excellence of his technique but because God has shown him the interpretation of the dream. Cf. 41.28: 'What God will do he has revealed to Pharaoh.' See above, pp. 49ff. Cf. B. Meissner, *op. cit.*, ii,

their skill essentially resided. The problem which the king poses is a darker mystery (*rāz*)[1] upon which only the God of heaven with whom light dwells can throw light (2.19, 20). We can see here the dependence of the epistemology of Jewish apocalyptic on this esoteric type of international wisdom, but we see no less clearly how the latter has been accommodated to the demands of Jewish piety.[2] The piety of Daniel is exemplified in his observance of dietary laws (1.8–16), in his psalm to the God of heaven[3] (2.20–23), in his persistent prayer to God in defiance of a royal edict (ch. 6), and in his confession of sin on behalf of himself and his people (9.3–19). His first allegiance is to God and he will not interrupt his prayer life for any royal edict, preferring a den of lions to the merest suggestion of temporization or apostasy.

Further a connection is established between his piety and the powers of illumination and insight with which he is endowed. Gabriel says to him: 'O Daniel, I have come to give you the capacity for perspicacity (*lehaśkīlekā bīnā*). At the beginning of your supplication a word (sc. from God) issued (sc. to me) . . . So see clearly into the word and have insight into the vision' (9.22–23, cf. 10.1). And God says to him: 'Do not be afraid, O Daniel, for from the first day that you set your mind to possess insight (*lehābīn*) and to humble yourself before your God your words were heard and I have come because of your words . . . and I come to give you insight (*lahabīnekā*) into what will befall your people at the end of days' (10.12–14). Daniel's prayerful and humble disposition is itself a mark of his *bīnā* and God comes in response to his prayers to confer *bīnā* on him.[4]

The element of enigma or riddle is even more strongly emphasized in the account which is given of Daniel's own visions and dreams in the later chapters of the book. Thus he has need of an

---

pp. 243, 264. Meissner notes that dreams were regarded as important omens, because it was believed that in them the gods made significant communications to men. They could, however, be dark and enigmatic and so a special class of *bārū* priest, an 'interpreter of dreams' (*pāšir sunāti*) was required to elucidate them.

[1] W. Baumgartner, *Lexicon, s.v. rāz*. A loan word from Persian.

[2] Similarly in the representation of Joseph as a dream interpreter. See above, p. 49, and cf. E. R. Ehrlich, *Der Traum im Alten Testament* (BZAW 73, 1953), pp. 122–3.

[3] See above, p. 34. This circumlocution for Yahweh is therefore a link with post-exilic Jewish legal piety. Cf. the references to the *tōrā* of Moses in Dan. 9.11, 13.

[4] Cf. Ps. 51.8 [6]: 'In secret (Köhler, "secretly") thou divulgest wisdom to me.'

angelic interpreter[1] to make the details of his visions luminous and intelligible (7.16). When he has seen a vision he searches for *bīnā* and Gabriel comes to give him insight (*hāḇēn*) into the vision and to divulge (*hinᵉnī mōḏīʿᵃḵā*) its meaning (8.16, 17, 19). Even so Daniel is still mesmerized (*wāʾeštōmēm*) and lacks clarity of comprehension (*ʾēn mēḇīn*, 8.27). After God has sought to enlighten him (*lahᵃḇīnᵉḵā*, 10.14), Daniel seeks further enlightenment from an angelic interpreter (12.6) and even then he says: 'But as for me I heard but I had no insight' (*wᵉlōʾ ʾāḇīn*, 12.8).

Thus we are in a very different theological atmosphere from that of Old Testament prophecy. God no longer declares his *ʿēṣā* plainly through the *dāḇār* of his prophet, but his communications are hidden in the riddle-like contents of visions and dreams and are unintelligible except to those who have been initiated into their mysteries. The prophet has been replaced by the interpreter who, in virtue of his God-given *bīnā*, can crack the code in which God conceals his detailed plans for the future, and so has the same powers of exact prediction as the Babylonian specialists claimed to possess through their closely guarded techniques. Such a one as Daniel is a *maśkīl* who can give insight (*yāḇīn*) to the many (11.33)[2] and illumine for them the dark sayings of God.

This seems to me to come near to the idea of an *élite*, composed of those who have direct insight into the veiled communications of God. On a lower level than this spiritual aristocracy are the 'many' whose knowledge of these mysteries can come only through the interpretation communicated to them by the *maśkīlīm*. It is true that we may have to reckon with the element of political expediency which may be operative in the eschewing of transparency and the calculated opaqueness of the medium. Perhaps connected with this also are the injunctions to secrecy—the *gnosis* is not to be broadcast (cf. 8.26, 12.9); the words are locked up and sealed until the time of the end. That is to say they are hidden with God and those who have access to his secrets. Yet the apocalyptist has something in common with the prophet. Wisdom and power still belong

[1] See above, p. 60, n. 1.

[2] Cf. 11.35; 12.3, 10 and notice the evidence of legal piety in these passages. The *maśkīlīm* are those who suffer vicariously in order to purge and purify the many (11.35). In 12.3 they are equated with those who justify the many (*maṣdīqē hārabbīm*) and in 12.10 they are the opposite of *rᵉšāʿīm*. None of the *rᵉšāʿīm* will be illumined, but the *maśkīlīm* will be illumined (*yāḇīnū*).

to God (2.20) and even as the *'ēṣā* expressed in the prophetic word would not fail of implementation, so the dream of the apocalyptist is reliable and its interpretation veracious (2.45).[1]

[1] Cf. E. R. Ehrlich, *op. cit.*, pp. 122–3. On the employment of the dream and its interpretation in the scheme of apocalyptic Ehrlich says: 'The symbol of the dream replaces the word of God. . . . The charismatically endowed dream-interpreter has to arrive at the meaning from these symbols and so, as he declares it, the future takes shape.'

IX

JEREMIAH AND PRE-EXILIC LEGAL PIETY

'How can you say: "We are *ḥakāmīm* and the *tōrā* of Yahweh is with us?" But, behold, the false pen of the *sōperīm* has falsified it (i.e. the *tōrā*). The *ḥakāmīm* shall be put to shame, they shall be broken to pieces and taken. Behold, they have rejected the *dābār* of Yahweh and what wisdom do they have?' (Jer. 8.8–9).[1]

The commentators tend not to pay sufficient attention to these references to *ḥakāmīm* and *sōperīm* and to explain them in too general a way. Thus Weiser[2] connects 8.8–9 with 8.4ff. and says that the *ḥakāmīm* are those who believe themselves not to be in need of the instruction which the prophet imparts. Hence Jeremiah's polemic is not directed in a precise way against wisdom and its practitioners, but is a general condemnation of the entire sacrificial law, and so is to be associated with 7.21. The essence of the covenant cult was a 'word of God', an oral recital of the *Heilsgeschichte* and the Decalogue, and a statement of the obligations of response in which the covenant people were involved. Jeremiah is here condemning all sacrificial and ceremonial prescriptions, those in the Book of the Covenant and Deuteronomy as well as those which were later codified in the priestly document.

Somewhat similar is the position of Hyatt.[3] He says that the *tōrā* of Jer. 8.8–9 probably included the Book of the Covenant and later codes such as H and P as well as Deuteronomy. Jeremiah here opposes the claim that the *tōrā* of Yahweh is contained in some written book or books and declares this *tōrā* false because it conflicts with the *dābār* of Yahweh. But there is a *tōrā* to which Yahweh adheres ('my *tōrā*', 6.19, 26.4), and this is to be equated

[1] There is no doubt that Jer. 8.8–9 stands apart from the other prophetic passages in which the *ḥakāmīm* are attacked. There they are statesmen or politicians, but here they are legal scholars (cf. Jer. 2.8, *tōpeśē hattōrā*). So J. Lindblom, 'Wisdom in the Old Testament Prophets', p. 195. See above, p. 38.

[2] A. Weiser, *Der Prophet Jeremia* (ATD 20, 1952), *in loc.*

[3] J. P. Hyatt, 'Torah in the Book of Deuteronomy', *JBL* 60 (1941), pp. 381–96.

with the ethical requirements and the prohibition against the worship of other gods which had been given to Israel in the desert by Moses. With this is contrasted the ritualistic requirements put forward by the priests (cf. 6.20) and the dependence on the existence of the temple for salvation.

This antithesis of ethical and sacrificial or ceremonial also appears in Duhm[1] who, however, identifies the *tōrā* of Jer. 8.8 with Deuteronomy. Jeremiah objected to the elaboration of the Book of the Covenant in the interests of Deuteronomic cultic theory and practice. While Jeremiah understood *mišpāṭ* as an assertion of the sovereignty of morality, the Deuteronomist had arrived at a system of *mišpāṭīm* which, in part, had quite a different intention—they were statements of correct sacrificial procedure. This, says Duhm, was an opiate which lulled the people into a false sense of security and encouraged them to believe that a correct temple cult was their guarantee of salvation. The *ḥakāmīm* or *sōperīm* are then, in Duhm's opinion, the Deuteronomic draftsmen and it is in virtue of their elaboration of a cultic theory that they are so called.

Whether or not Duhm is correct in equating the *tōrā* of Jer. 8.8 with Deuteronomy[2] is a question to which I feel unable to give a positive answer, but, having made this equation, Duhm does not make the best use of it and draws what I think is the wrong conclusion. Why should it be assumed that the *ḥakāmīm* who are mentioned in 8.8–9 only acquire this title as sophisticated theorists in connection with the drafting of Deuteronomy? These verses seem to me rather to point to a relationship between Deuteronomy and the practitioners of the wisdom literature, assuming the correctness of Duhm's equation.

What we would then learn from 8.8–9 is that the literary presentation of the cultic theory of Deuteronomy was shaped in those circles which were professionally associated with the transmission and teaching of the wisdom literature. Irrespective, however, of

[1] B. Duhm, *Das Buch Jeremia* (KHKAT, 1901), *in loc.*

[2] Cf. G. Östborn, *op. cit.*, p. 53. Östborn argues that the ultimate equation of *tōrā* with Law comes about because the Law is a didactic instrument whose function is to provide 'instruction'. Hence *tōrā* comes to be used not only of instruction based on the Law but of the Law itself. Östborn believes that this concern with the teaching or imparting of the Law is best illustrated by Deuteronomy, but he also cites Ex. 24.12. When Yahweh writes down the Law and gives it to Moses it is to the end that it should be an instrument of instruction (*lehōrōṯām*).

the correctness of Duhm's equation of *tōrā* in 8.8–9 with Deuteronomy, there is evidence within the book of Deuteronomy itself of an intention to present its theory and demands as the true wisdom.[1]

Rudolph's[2] exegesis does not bite into the problems of 8.8–9 any more than the work of the commentators just reviewed. He says simply that *tōrā* refers to a written law whose guardians were the priests (hence he equates *tōpᵉśē hattōrā* in 2.8 with the priests)[3] and that they are called *ḥᵃḵāmīm* as writers of this *tōrā*, i.e. as *sōpᵉrīm*. At this stage, he holds, the *sōpēr*, as a scholar of the *tōrā*, is not the occupant of a separate office and cannot be distinguished from the priest in the way which is possible in post-exilic Judaism.[4] Otherwise his exegesis follows familiar lines and Jeremiah's polemic is thought to be against the distortion of the true *tōrā* (i.e. the moral demands of the Decalogue) through the undue emphasis which is placed on cultic matters.

Volz[5] comes to grips in a more determined way with the questions raised by these verses. He equates the *tōpᵉśē hattōrā* of 2.8 with the *ḥᵃḵāmīm* and *sōpᵉrīm* of 8.8–9 and identifies them with the forerunners of the post-exilic wisdom teachers and scholars of the Law. Hence Volz does not identify the *tōpᵉśē hattōrā* of 2.8 or the *ḥᵃḵāmīm* and *sōpᵉrīm* of 8.8–9 absolutely with the priests, although he says that these men were related to the priests in station and calling.[6] They were luminaries who gave advice on the written and unwritten law and who probably also imparted instruction in the *tōrā* to the young. Jeremiah's quarrel with them arises from the circumstance that they claim divine authority for their legal rulings, which he regards as no more than human opinions.

With this should be compared Lindblom's statement: 'Thus "the wise" are the people who have devoted themselves to the study of these laws and present themselves as instructors of the people in questions pertaining to the law and the application of its

[1] Cf. J. Lindblom, 'Wisdom in the Old Testament Prophets', p. 195. 'It seems as though the emergence of this class of wise men coincided with the appearance of Deuteronomy. They call themselves "Wise". This designation is dependent on the claim of Deuteronomy itself (4.6) to contain the true wisdom.'

[2] W. Rudolph, *Jeremia*² (HAT 12, 1958), *in loc.*

[3] Similarly B. Duhm. Also F. Giesebrecht, *Das Buch Jeremia* (HKAT, 1894), *in loc.*

[4] Similarly J. Lindblom, 'Wisdom in the Old Testament Prophets', p. 196.

[5] P. Volz, *Der Prophet Jeremia* (KAT, 1922), *in loc.*

[6] Similarly G. Östborn, *op. cit.*, p. 109, and J. P. Hyatt, 'Torah in the Book of Jeremiah', p. 386 ('probably a subdivision of the priesthood'). Cf. A. Bentzen, *Introduction* i, p. 216.

rules to practical life.'[1] Östborn's position resembles that of Lindblom in that he stops short of equating the *ḥᵃkāmîm* of 8.8–9 with the class of the 'Wise'. He says: 'I hold that the *tōpᵉśê hattōrā* and the *sōpᵉrîm* of Jeremiah 2.8 and 8.8 refer to some kind of scholars or teachers of the Law standing in close contact with the Wise Men.'[2] Hyatt[3] says of the *sōpᵉrîm* of 8.8–9 that they were more than copyists; they were concerned not merely with writing down the *tōrā* but also with its interpretation and even with creating *tōrōṯ*. Their emergence is to be traced to the need for legal interpreters created by the publication of Deuteronomy.

Volz along with Giesebrecht, Rudolph and Weiser rejects the view that 8.8–9 refers to Deuteronomy, but Volz goes farther than the others in denying that the protest has anything to do with cultic codification. It is not the antithesis of ethical and cultic on which Jeremiah's attack hinges, but the antithesis of the absolutely authoritative prophetic *dāḇār* and the merely human, legal opinions of the *ḥᵃkāmîm*. He objects to their practice of writing down their rulings and giving them the status and authority of legal definitions by attributing them to Yahweh.

The deficiency in Volz's account and in the related accounts of Lindblom and Östborn is that not enough attention is paid to the appearance of *ḥᵃkāmîm* and *ḥoḵmā* in 8.8–9. It is true that these *ḥᵃkāmîm* are on the way to becoming legal scholars[4] and Giesebrecht and Volz are right in seeing here the evidence of pre-exilic legal piety, so that it ought not to be supposed that Ezra was a *sōpēr* on an entirely new model and that he had no forerunners in pre-exilic Judah. But we have also to ask ourselves in what tradition these *ḥᵃkāmîm* or *sōpᵉrîm* stood. They belong to the tradition of international wisdom.

We have already met the *sōpēr* as a Secretary of State[5] and the *ḥᵃkāmîm* against whom Isaiah and Jeremiah inveigh in the other passages which we have examined were influential statesmen.[6] I

[1] J. Lindblom, 'Wisdom in the Old Testament Prophets', p. 195.

[2] G. Östborn, *op. cit.*, p. 112.

[3] J. P. Hyatt, *op. cit.*, p. 384.

[4] Cf. A. Bentzen, *Introduction*, i, p. 216. Bentzen remarks that 2.8 and 8.8–9 testify to an incipient differentiation which ultimately led to the establishment of the class of the *nomikoi*. He continues: 'In this development the activity of the sages of the wisdom literature may have been of importance.'

[5] See above, pp. 17ff.

[6] See above, pp. 65ff.

have tried to explain, however, that diversity of function is a characteristic which must be expected of the *ḥāḵām* or *sōp̄ēr*.[1] These men belonged to an educated class whose mental habits were shaped by a common educational discipline and they have the basic intellectual equipment for positions of power and responsibility in the community. The pattern of this education was particularly orientated towards the needs of the state for higher civil servants, but the bench[2] would require some of these *ḥᵃḵāmîm*, while the temple would get its share, since it needed both administrators and scholars to advance sacred learning.

It is probable that the *ḥᵃḵāmîm* or *sōp̄ᵉrîm* mentioned in 8.8–9 were wisdom teachers and that Jeremiah is pointing to what was for them a significant change of occupation. The 'nationalization' of international wisdom was then already under way in the pre-exilic period and the *ḥᵃḵāmîm* were emerging as apologists of the Law and were engaged in literary activities with a view to presenting the Law as the true wisdom. That there was such a development in pre-exilic times is denied by Lindblom, who says: 'In earlier times there existed no intimate relationship between the Torah and the Wise, as representatives of wisdom in a special sense. A change came about in post-exilic times. The Torah was then regarded as the epitome of all wisdom and the teaching in the wisdom schools manifestly also included instruction in the principles and commands of the Law.'[3]

What Lindblom appears to overlook is that it was always the business of the *ḥᵃḵāmîm* to impart 'instruction' and that *tôrā* was an item of the vocabulary of wisdom (Prov. 1.8; 3.1; 6.20, 23; 7.2; 13.14; 31.26) prior to the flowing together of Law and Wisdom. It is not therefore an innovation for the *ḥᵃḵāmîm* to deal in *tôrā*, but the new element in the situation is their acceptance of the equation of *tôrā* with Law. For the *ḥᵃḵāmîm* therefore what is involved is a redefinition of *tôrā*[4] by accepting which they make their bow to a distinctively Israelite concept of Law and so to a legal, Yahwistic piety.[5]

[1] See above, pp. 23ff.
[2] Cf. B. Gemser, *Sprüche Salomos*, p. 49.
[3] J. Lindblom, 'Wisdom in the Old Testament Prophets', p. 196.
[4] See above, p. 103, n. 2.
[5] Cf. M. Noth, 'Die Gesetze im Pentateuch', *Gesammelte Studien zum Alten Testament* (1957), pp. 9–141. Noth points out (pp. 32–53) that Old Testament Law presupposes a community whose God is Yahweh and whose connection with his

Thus it seems to me that it is a *literary* activity[1] of the *ḥᵃkāmīm* to which Jeremiah is referring—their emergence as apologists for the *tōrā*—rather than their canonizing of *ad hoc* legal rulings as Volz supposes. Jeremiah is describing a new phenomenon—the first stages in the reinterpretation of Wisdom in terms of Law. In a limited sense this process might also be described as the invasion of Law by Wisdom. This is true to the extent that these learned apologists imported into the *tōrā* the vocabulary and forms of the wisdom literature.[2]

Whatever interpretation is placed on Jer. 8.8–9 there are independent indications in the book of Deuteronomy of an intention to present the Law as the true wisdom. Thus in Deut. 4.5–6 Israel is commanded to keep the *ḥuqqīm* and *mišpāṭīm* of Yahweh in the land of Canaan and these are said to be her *ḥokmā* and *bīnā* in the sight of all nations who will say when they hear all these *ḥuqqīm*: 'Surely this great nation is a people *ḥāḵām* and *nāḇōn*.' Here the vocabulary of old wisdom is reinterpreted in terms of Deuteronomic piety.

Again in Deut. 29.8 [9] Moses says to Israel: 'Keep the words of the covenant (i.e. the *bᵉrīṯ* between Yahweh and Israel which, according to Deuteronomy, was renewed in Moab) in order that you may act with competence (*taśkīlū*) in all that you do.' So competence or grasp is no longer an intellectual virtue within the framework of a critical, empirical statecraft, but is derived from a correct religious posture.

In this connection I call attention to Weinfeld's[3] argument that a humanist tone pervades Deuteronomy and that the aim of the author(s) is to explain and instruct on the basis of ancient laws. 'The primary aim of the Deuteronomic author is the instruction of the people in humanism and, in furtherance of this goal, he adapts the various literary traditions which were at his disposal. The historical elements serve the author for instructional ends, while

---

people is grounded in past historical events. Law is therefore the expression of the exclusiveness of the relationship between Yahweh and Israel (pp. 67–81). It is in this sense that the submission of the *ḥᵃkāmīm* to Law and their literary portrayal of the Law as the true wisdom represents a 'nationalization' of wisdom.

[1] So G. Östborn, *op. cit.*, p. 109, who says that it appears from Jer. 8.8 that the *ḥᵃkāmīm* dealt with the *tōrā* in a written form.

[2] The part of the argument dealing with the presence of Wisdom forms in Law cannot be pursued in this work, but I hope to return to it at a future date.

[3] M. Weinfeld, 'The Origin of the Humanism in Deuteronomy', *JBL* 80 (1961), pp. 241–7.

the law serves to concretize the moral and humanist principles which are his educational goals.'[1]

Hence Weinfeld argues that Deuteronomy represents the fusion of law and wisdom rather than of law and prophecy and that the author makes a selective use of the laws, omitting those which have no great importance for his humanist principles and deriving certain of his prescriptions from the wisdom literature. Weinfeld thus reverses the conclusions of other scholars who have noted connections between Deuteronomy and the wisdom literature and have concluded that the dependence is on the side of the latter, for he asserts that it is Deuteronomy itself which has assimilated 'ancient wisdom elements'.[2] It will be noted that Weinfeld's thesis is in general agreement with the arguments which I have developed in this section concerning the connections of the *ḥᵃḵāmīm* with pre-exilic legal piety. Weinfeld tends to see this as an invasion of Law by the humanist tradition of Wisdom, but it is also and more significantly, as I have pointed out, the subjugation of Wisdom to Law.

A few Deuteronomic passages from other books can also be drawn into the argument. In Josh. 1.7–8 Yahweh commands Joshua to be careful to act in agreement with all that Moses commanded (or, in agreement with all that the *tōrā* of Moses commanded) in order that he may act with competence (*taśkīl*) in every place where he goes. In Josh. 1.8 the reference to the *tōrā* is certain. By taking care to observe all that is written in it Joshua will prosper in his way and show competence. Hence competence or grasp (*śeḵel*) is now traced to a knowledge of the *tōrā* and obedience to its demands. Very close to this is I Kings 2.3, where David enjoins Solomon to keep the charge of God, to walk in his ways and to keep his statutes, ordinances and directives (*'ēḏōṯ*) according as it is written in the *tōrā* of Moses, 'in order that you may show competence (*taśkīl*) in all that you do and in all to which you turn'. In these three passages the practical orientation of *śkl*—its association with the management of affairs—is retained, only such grasp or efficiency is now represented as flowing from legal piety.

The descriptions in the book of Kings of the wisdom of

[1] *Op. cit.*, pp. 242–3.
[2] *Ibid.*, pp. 245–7.

Solomon are also accommodated to a similar piety (cf. I Kings 3.3). In a night dream Yahweh appears to Solomon (I.3.5, 15) and they converse together. Solomon confesses his lack of political know-how and his inadequate grasp of affairs (I.3.7). *Lēḇ*, which in the context of old wisdom means 'mind' or 'mental grasp'[1] and is a matter of native wits and educational discipline, is here the gift of Yahweh and is given in answer to prayer. Thus Solomon's legal acumen (*lēḇ šōmēaʿ*, I.3.9) and discrimination (*hāḇīn*, I.3.9, 11) are bestowed by Yahweh, who gives him a *lēḇ* which is *ḥāḵām* and *nāḇōn* (I.3.12).[2] Also in I Kings 5.9 [4.29]ff. Solomon's *ḥoḵmā*, *teḇūnā* and *rōḥab lēb*[3] are the gift of God and this is why he far outreaches the sages of Edom and Egypt.[4]

There are one or two passages in the book of Psalms where the vocabulary of wisdom appears in a similar framework of legal piety. In Ps. 119.98–100 the psalmist traces his superior wisdom to the commandments (*miṣwōṯ*) of Yahweh. Because he occupies his mind with the authoritative statements or directives (*ʿēḏōṯ*) of Yahweh, he has more grasp than his teachers, and because he keeps the charges of Yahweh (*piqqūḏīm*), he is more perspicacious (*'eṯbōnān*) than the elders. That is to say *ḥoḵmā, śeḵel* and *teḇūnā* are not to be learned from a teacher who has digested the accumulated experience of many generations of wise men and who imparts this to his pupils, nor from a *zāqēn* who instructs out of the experience of a long life. Wisdom is not an empirical art; it is Yahweh's illumination of the mind through the *tōrā*.

And so Ps. 19.8 [7] says that the raw youth (*peṯī*)[5] who has no experience of life and whose mental habits have not been formed by the discipline of empirical wisdom is made wise by the directives (*ʿēḏōṯ*) of Yahweh. It is not my intention to claim that these passages from the psalms are pre-exilic, but I cite them because they show how the vocabulary of wisdom was used in connection

[1] See above, pp. 15–16.
[2] Cf. I Kings 5.18 [4] ff.; 10.24; Deut. 4.6.
[3] The antithesis of *ḥasar lēḇ*, 'mentally deficient'.
[4] Cf. M. Noth, 'Die Bewährung von Salomos "Göttlicher Weisheit" '. Noth suggests that this mode of divine guidance should be contrasted with the guidance which is afforded through the oracle. It is divine wisdom and the gift of God, 'but yet it is now in Solomon, it is his possession with which he can work and it makes it unnecessary to consult God with regard to the details of the verdict' (p. 232). It may be that this concept of divine guidance, representing as it does a reinterpretation of the vocabulary of wisdom, was more congenial to legal piety than the oracle.
[5] Arabic *fattā*, 'a youth', hence one who is inexperienced, unsophisticated, raw.

with the presentation of the *tōrā* as the true wisdom and, in this respect, are a continuation of a process which had already begun in the late pre-exilic period.

The representation that wisdom derives from an endowment of the spirit is also, in my opinion, exilic or post-exilic. I agree with those who conclude from the expression in Isa. 11.1 that 11.1–9 comes from a period when the Davidic monarchy had been suppressed and Judah had lost her political independence.[1] The passage therefore is exilic and it is relevant to this enquiry because the ideal Davidic king is portrayed in the vocabulary of wisdom as a sage. His wisdom is to derive from a charismatic endowment (the *rūaḥ* of Yahweh will rest upon him) and is associated with piety (even legal piety)—the fear of Yahweh (*yirʾaṯ YHWH*). His endowment is further delineated as a *rūaḥ* of *ḥoḵmā* and *bīnā*, a *rūaḥ* of policy (*ʿēṣā*) and power (*geḇūrā*), a *rūaḥ* of knowledge and the fear of Yahweh (v. 2).

Thus he possesses all the virtues of thought and action associated with an able king, but these have been strangely transformed. His mind is illumined by the spirit of Yahweh, he is disciplined by the fear of Yahweh and his power is in the sceptre of his mouth and the breath of his lips (v. 4).[2] Moreover, his wisdom and power are committed on the side of righteousness. When he sits to hear legal cases he pierces below the surface of things and does not administer correction by hearsay. He takes pains to ensure that the poor and the weak are not at a disadvantage in the court.

Another late passage with a similar type of representation is Neh. 9.20. In the wilderness Yahweh gave the Israelites his good spirit (*rūḥaḵā haṭṭōḇā*) in order to confer competence upon them (*lehaśkîlām*). Also Deut. 34.9, according to which Joshua was full of the spirit of wisdom (*rūaḥ ḥoḵmā*), because Moses had laid his hands upon him. Hence he is a *ḥāḵām* because he is in the prophetic succession and *ḥoḵmā* is a charisma.[3]

I take up again the main thread of the discussion and I ask the

[1] Most recently J. Lindblom, *Prophecy in Ancient Israel*, pp. 368, 394. Cf. J. Fichtner, 'Jesaja unter den Weisen', cols. 78–79, who supposes that 11.1–9 are to be attributed to Isaiah of Jerusalem and are part of the evidence that he was once a wisdom teacher.

[2] Cf. J. Fichtner, *ibid.*, col. 79. 'But the expected king of God's people, furnished with the spirit of Yahweh, will reign with divine wisdom.'

[3] See above, p. 16, on Ex. 28.3 (P.), where the craftsman's skill is an endowment of the spirit.

question why Jeremiah's attitude to the reinterpretation of wisdom in terms of legal piety should have been so hostile. Duhm[1] speaks finely about the perils of codification and a religion of the book. It is, he says, the tragedy of religion that the dead prophets slay those who are yet alive in the sense which Jesus intended when he said: 'Alas, you build the tombs of the prophets whom your fathers murdered, and so testify that you approve of the deeds your fathers did; they committed the murders and you provide the tombs' (Luke 11.47–48, NEB). In other words those who venerate the prophets who are dead are one in spirit with those who rejected them while they were alive and were offended by their words. Veneration is less costly than obedience. I think that Duhm is partly right in seeing here a conflict between the living, prophetic word and the written, normative code which is always a century or two behind the times.

There remains, however, the particular circumstance that in 8.8–9 Jeremiah taxes the *ḥᵃkāmīm* or *sōpᵉrīm* with falsehood or fraud, and so we have to ask ourselves what it was he saw of a fraudulent or spurious character in their presentation of the Law as the true wisdom. It would have been reasonable to suppose that he might have welcomed this reinterpretation of wisdom in terms of Law as a sign of regeneration in the *ḥᵃkāmim*. Most of the prophetic criticisms of wisdom are directed against the assumptions of a pragmatic, self-contained *'ēṣā* which had no room for piety in its system. But against this wisdom which has surrendered to the Law Jeremiah levels the same charge that he had made against the pragmatic wisdom of statecraft—it is a rejection of the *dāḇār* of Yahweh of which the prophet is the bearer.

We have considered in some detail in what sense the old wisdom amounted to a rejection of the *dāḇār* of Yahweh, but how can the same be said of this wisdom which has made its bow to the Law? The precise reference of the allegation that the false pen of the *sōpᵉrīm* had falsified the *tōrā* is perhaps to the use made by these *ḥᵃkāmīm* or *sōpᵉrīm* of the vocabulary of wisdom and of explanatory expansions after the manner of the wisdom literature. This was how they set about their literary work as apologists for the Law. In their presentation of it they employed the vocabulary and the forms of the wisdom literature.

[1] *Op. cit., in loc.*

More generally Jeremiah was convinced that this effort at reinterpretation, whereby wisdom was brought into the fold of legal piety, was essentially bogus and did not constitute an authentic response to the *dāḇār* of Yahweh. It had too much of the character of pen and paper work; it too much resembled an ingenious academic exercise and was lacking in passion and high relevance. It was the bookish accomplishment of scholars who were making their bow to the orthodoxy of the Law, but it had been carried out in the seclusion of an ivory tower by men who were remote from the sterner realities of existence, who did not know the agony of exposure to crisis or the *dāḇār* of Yahweh which issued from such passionate involvement.

To a man like Jeremiah, immersed in contemporary conflict and convinced that Yahweh's *dāḇār* spoke of the imminent dissolution of the Judaean state and the destruction of the temple, such labours were trivial and spurious. And, if 8.8–9 indeed refers to Deuteronomy, we must see in it an anguished protest against the false sense of security which was encouraged by the dogma of centralization, for the temple was not the ground nor guarantee of Jerusalem's inviolability and it must not be supposed that a striving after cultic propriety would stave off the disaster threatened by the *dāḇār* of Yahweh.

X

CONCLUSION

My intention here is not so much to say anything new as to draw out the implications of the argument which has been developed in the earlier part of this work. I have examined in some detail the use made of the vocabulary of wisdom by Isaiah and Jeremiah and I shall illustrate what I have to say in this general conclusion with reference to these two prophets.

We are told in Isa. 7 (II Kings 16.5ff.) how the prophet sought out an interview with Ahaz in order to offer him advice on a matter of prime political urgency. The cause of this crisis was the determination of Syria and Israel to use force if necessary in order to bring Judah into a coalition and to replace Ahaz with a more pliant king.[1] The object of this projected alliance was, in all probability, to offer resistance to the Assyrian advance into the area of Syria-Palestine.

The gist of Isaiah's advice was that Ahaz should not be intimidated by the threats of the two neighbouring kings and that he should not embark on any extraordinary diplomatic measures in order to counter Syro-Ephraimite pressure. The *'ēṣā* of Syria and Ephraim will not be implemented (*lō' ṯāqūm wᵉlō' ṯihye*).[2] Fichtner[3] suggests that Isa. 8.10 should be associated with 7.5ff. In spite of all their preparations for war, the nations will be crushed by Yahweh. 'Formulate a policy (*'ēṣā*) and it will be nullified (*wᵉṯūpār*); speak a word, but it will not be implemented (*wᵉlō' ṯāqūm*).' There is perhaps in this language an implied contrast between the *'ēṣā* which will fail and the prophetic *dāḇār* which, bearing the authority of Yahweh, must come to fruition.

Instead of following Isaiah's advice to keep calm and face the

[1] Cf. E. Würthwein, 'Jesaja 7.1–9. Ein Beitrag zu dem Thema: Prophetie und Politik', *Theologie als Glaubenswagnis* (Karl Heim Festschrift), 1954. Würthwein argues (pp. 47–50) that the threat was particularly directed against Ahaz.

[2] Isa. 7.5, 7.

[3] J. Fichtner, 'Jahves Plan in der Botschaft des Jesaja', p. 22.

demands of the two kings with unwavering resistance,[1] Ahaz made his submission to Tiglath-Pileser, sent him a present of silver and gold and asked him to intervene on behalf of Judah so as to remove the threat of invasion by her two northern neighbours.

There are one or two features of this episode which invite comment. Ahaz is faced with the threat of invasion and so the interview takes place at a moment when the safety of the Judaean state hangs in the balance and the king is confronted with a decision of the greatest delicacy and gravity. Yet it is just here—in this area of crucial political decision—that the prophet intervenes and tenders his advice. The prophet, as Yahweh's spokesman, cannot avoid interfering in affairs of state and seeking to influence the policies of the king and his high political advisers, because the most important things which he has to say deal with just those matters.

Würthwein[2] argues that for Isaiah the issue is Yahweh's covenant or the pact with Assyria—a pact which presupposed the recognition of foreign gods. Würthwein acutely observes that the discrepancy between such 'covenant thinking' and the *Realpolitik* of the statesmen of Judah would reveal itself especially in such a situation of crisis as Judah now faced. He elucidates 7.1ff. with special reference to the covenant between the Davidic dynasty and Yahweh. Isaiah's words are addressed to the king and his house in particular and not to the people as a whole and vv. 7–9 are an 'actualization' of the prediction of Nathan in II Sam. 7.16. This is the crux of Isaiah's debate with Ahaz and his demand is that the king's attitudes and actions at all times must demonstrate that this covenant is for him the deepest reality that he knows, on which his existence and that of Judah depends.

If the content of the *dāḇār* which the prophet speaks normally belonged to an area of concern and decision different from that of the statesman, then prophet and statesman might co-exist happily, each satisfied with a convenient allocation of spheres of influence.

[1] So E. Würthwein, *op. cit.*, pp. 50–52. Würthwein holds that Isaiah's speech is related in form (*Gattung*) to the war-speech of Deut. 20.2–4. It is not pacifism or a recommendation to do nothing, but is advice to resist the two kings with calm and fearlessness (*hašqēṭ* in 7.4 means 'a feeling of security'). It needs to be said, however, that this would appear no less 'unklug und für die wirklichen Verhältnisse unbrauchbar' to the king's professional advisers than pure pacifism (cf. H. Gressmann, *Der Messias* [1929], p. 238, n. 1).

[2] E. Würthwein, *op. cit.*, pp. 56–63.

But, if they both tender advice—advice which conflicts and which derives from incompatible fundamental presuppositions—on the same life-and-death matters of state, a very uncomfortable and even dangerous situation is created both for the statesman and the prophet. For now the prophet is entering what the statesman believes to be his preserve and is challenging the authority and validity of well-tried and universally recognized crafts of political negotiation and diplomacy.

What Ahaz refused to do was just to abandon the well-charted routes of political negotiation and in this he would certainly have the backing of his professional advisers. Was he to scrap the ways of thinking and the attitudes which were universally current in diplomatic exchanges and political bargaining and to base the security of Judah on trust in Yahweh? We should not underestimate the revolutionary character of this demand nor wonder that the statesmen boggled at it and were moved to consternation and anger when it was formulated by a prophet of Yahweh. Conversely we can see that because Isaiah and Jeremiah rejected the basic assumptions of international diplomacy—because they denied that the historical process was a power struggle—they had no time for foreign alliances or for political bargaining which aimed at securing the maximum advantage for Judah in the contest for power between the great nations.[1]

The decision of the statesmen to negotiate a pact with Egypt no doubt rested on careful political calculations. Those who initiated this policy believed that their timing was impeccable and that this was a brilliant diplomatic stroke which would release Judah from

[1] J. Fichtner, 'Jesaja unter den Weisen', cols. 78–80, points to Isaiah's use of the *Gattungen* (parables, wisdom-sentences) and the vocabulary of wisdom and asks how it is that the prophet occupies so ambivalent a position, being at once an opponent of wisdom and a disciple of wisdom. He explains this by assuming that Isaiah was a wisdom teacher before his call to be a prophet. He was one of the men of Hezekiah (Prov. 25–29), but out of the experience of his call it became clear to him that he had to sever himself from worldly, self-contained wisdom and to undertake the particular task of proclaiming that men, for all their human wisdom, could not grasp his message, although they might hear it (Isa. 6.9ff.) Note especially *wᵉʾal tāḇînû* in v.9 and *yāḇîn* in v. 10. Fichtner offers an interesting explanation of 28.9–10. The prophet's opponents are sneering at his earlier occupation, which was well known to them. Will he teach us ABC's? Will he treat us as if we were children? Cf. R. J. Anderson, 'Was Isaiah a Scribe?' *JBL* 79 (1960), pp. 57–58. Anderson suggests that Isaiah was a royal counsellor in the reign of Uzziah, a prophet of the 'unsolicited judgment of Yahweh' in the reign of Ahaz and then again the adviser of Hezekiah, although at the time of Isa. 38.1–7 'he had not yet been rehired on the official staff'. This is fanciful.

the grip of Assyria. They argued that Egypt was on the ascendant and would soon be the dominant power and that now was the time for Judah to defy Assyria and to throw in her lot with Egypt. If she could get good terms from Egypt now, she would reap the benefit of this bold diplomatic initiative when Egypt had replaced Assyria as her suzerain. All the assumptions of this political strategy are rejected outright by Isaiah, as has already been shown by the examination of those passages which deal with the projected pact[1] (Isa. 30.1–7; 31.1–3; cf. Jer. 37.6ff.).

It is true that connivance and intrigue with Egypt should sometimes be seen as an instinctive and inveterate tendency rather than as deliberate political calculation. Here the physical adjacency of Judah to Egypt is an important influence and Noth[2] has remarked that Egypt was from 720 BC onwards the power behind all anti-Assyrian movements in Syria-Palestine. It should not, however, be supposed that after the defeat of Necho at Carchemish in 605 BC Egypt ceased to be a real alternative to Neo-Babylonian suzerainty, so that pro-Egyptian trends in Judah were now merely instinctive and irrational gestures and no longer made any political sense.

On this Wiseman[3] says that after Carchemish and in view of Nebuchadrezzar's annual expeditions to the west Necho concluded that he could not recover control of Syria by direct action and must remain within his own borders. On the successful Egyptian resistance to Nebuchadrezzar in 601 BC Wiseman says: 'The vigour of Egyptian defence in 601 BC agrees with what little is known of that country's history and policies during this period. It would show that the defeat at Carchemish was but a temporary loss of military strength, perhaps mainly affecting garrison troops.'[4] An Egyptian army did, in fact, come to the help of Zedekiah (Jer. 37.5; cf. 34.21), and at the time of the final siege of Jerusalem we hear from the Lachish Ostraka of a certain Kebaryahu or Konyahu, a

[1] See above, pp. 71ff.

[2] M. Noth, *History*, p. 262.

[3] D. J. Wiseman, *Chronicles of Chaldaean Kings (626–556 B.C.) in the British Museum* (1956), pp. 25ff.

[4] Similarly J. P. Hyatt, 'New Light on Nebuchudrezzar and Judean History', *JBL* 75 (1956), p. 282. Referring to the period subsequent to 605 BC, Hyatt says: 'It thus appears that Babylonia was somewhat weaker and Egypt somewhat stronger than has often been assumed. This helps to account for the frequent vacillations in Judean foreign policy during this era.' On the expeditions of Psammetichus II and Apries to Phoenicia, Wiseman comments: 'Egypt still aimed to expand towards Syria whenever the Babylonian hold there became weak' (*op. cit.*, p. 31).

supreme commander of the Jewish militia, who went down to Egypt presumably to get Egyptian help.[1]

However vexatious Isaiah's intervention, his advice to Ahaz was intended to be constructive and was in effect a guarantee from Yahweh that Judah was secure. The conflict between prophet and statesman does not assume its sharpest form until it calls in question the security of the state and amounts to a prediction of impending disaster and dissolution. Then the prophet's words take on in the minds of kings and statesmen their most dangerous and sinister shape, and it is clear that there was a period when Isaiah was prophesying destruction for Judah and Jerusalem (e.g. 10.11–12). He asserts that Assyria is Yahweh's instrument to work judgment on Jerusalem even as she has already accomplished this against Samaria, but that after the task of destroying Jerusalem is completed Yahweh will lay Assyria low.

But the prophetic word concerning Jerusalem is different at the moment when the army of Sennacherib is at the gates and her destruction seems inevitable. Here again, in a moment of dire peril for Judah, Isaiah addresses a message to the king and assures Hezekiah that Yahweh will preserve Jerusalem inviolate. Assyria has ceased to function as the rod of his anger and it is no part of Yahweh's purpose to permit the Assyrians to desecrate Jerusalem (ch. 37). And there is a constructive side to his denunciation of diplomatic activity directed towards Egypt in that he couples it with the assertion that Yahweh will protect Jerusalem (31.5). Thus Isaiah in company with the eighth-century prophets interpreted the advance of Assyria as the proof of Yahweh's determination to bring his own people to judgment, but he contradicted this doctrine at the point where he asserted that Jerusalem was inviolable from the Assyrian invader.

When Isaiah conveys this assurance to Hezekiah, he advances no reasons such as might have been required to win the credence of a practising statesman. He adduces none of the considerations which would appear to a statesman to be immediately relevant to

[1] H. Torczyner, *The Lachish Letters* (Lachish I), 1938, iii.13ff. Cf. M. Noth, *History*, p. 284. D. W. Thomas 'The Age of Jeremiah in the Light of Recent Archeological Discovery', *PEQ* (1950), p. 2. Thomas says that the object of Konyahu's mission remains obscure, but that with Zedekiah and his court so strongly pro-Egyptian, it is understandable that a military officer of high rank should have been sent at this time to Egypt to solicit help against the Babylonians.

any attempt to calculate the chances of Judah's survival. If she does survive with Sennacherib and his army at her gates, this will make nonsense of any careful assessment of historical probabilities. With Isaiah Jerusalem's survival is a doctrine deriving from his conviction that he speaks Yahweh's *dāḇār* and that Yahweh will take extraordinary measures to bring about the withdrawal of Sennacherib (37.7). But this is far removed from the accepted methods of calculating political security and would bring conviction only to those who shared the prophet's faith in Yahweh.

In the case of Jeremiah this conflict between prophet and statesman becomes intolerably sharp; the prophetic word is held to be treasonable, the prophet is subjected to violence and imprisonment and is threatened with death (36.26; 37.15, 20–21). Chapter 36 throws a particularly illuminating light on the attitude of the *śārīm* to the claim of the prophet to possess valid *ʿēṣā* as the bearer of the *dāḇār* of Yahweh.[1] Here an impressive line of commentators have concluded that the statesmen identify themselves absolutely in this chapter with the point of view of Jeremiah and that it is their intention to urge on Jehoiakim that Jeremiah's *ʿēṣā* has urgent political relevance and that it should be implemented as the only policy which can save the state from disaster.

Thus Rudolph,[2] commenting on 36.16, says that the *śārīm* were deeply moved when Baruch read the contents of his scroll to them and that they were men of a different stamp from the wanton and frivolous Jehoiakim. Rudolph supposes that the fear of the *śārīm* in 36.16 is a fear of the prophetic word and so implies the recognition of the authority of that word and the belief that it would certainly be fulfilled. According to this interpretation they interrogated Baruch in order to ascertain that the contents of the scroll had their source in a prophet before they went to report the affair to the king.

Similarly Volz[3] says that when the scroll was read to the statesmen in the cabinet room they were alarmed because of the divine threat just as Josiah had been alarmed (II Kings 22.11). Believing

[1] It is usually assumed that the defeat of Necho at Carchemish in 605 BC was the occasion of this renewed public appeal of Jeremiah. He nourished the hope that the mood of statesmen and people would now be sobered and chastened, and that they would be more receptive to his *ʿēṣā* than hitherto.

[2] W. Rudolph, *Jeremia²*, *in loc.*

[3] P. Volz, *Der Prophet Jeremia* (KAT, 1922), *in loc.*

the safety of the state to be jeopardized by the prophetic word, they considered it their duty to communicate with the king, in all probability with the intention of urging him to receive the prophetic warning favourably. On v. 19 Volz says that it is a testimony to the noble and courageous character of these officials that in such circumstances they went to the king without delay. Their concern for the well-being of their fatherland urged them on and they welcomed the opportunity to change the hard, self-willed disposition of the king.

Duhm[1] likewise remarks on the powerful impression which the reading of the scroll had on the *śārīm* and declares that their resolve to communicate with the king is an indication that they believed in the prophetic prediction and were anxious to apprise the king of the danger which threatened the state. The interrogation of Baruch was not inquisitorial; the *śārīm* did not regard the contents of the scroll as highly dangerous and treasonable, but they were anxious to establish that it contained authoritative prophetic words and Baruch assured them that every syllable was from Jeremiah.

Weiser[2] says that the *śārīm* recognized the urgency of the crisis given by God and had full understanding of and were completely sympathetic towards the intention of the new action of the prophet which was to initiate and urge a policy of repentance. It was in order to satisfy themselves that they had a watertight case to present to the king that they established through their interrogation of Baruch that Jeremiah was the source of the proclamation, for in that case they knew that behind it was the authority of Yahweh.

I am not convinced that this is a correct understanding of the attitude of the *śārīm* and all of these commentators are in some difficulty with 36.24. Duhm's[3] textual emendation may be taken to indicate that he is aware of a problem of interpretation in connection with this verse. The assumption of Volz and Rudolph that the *śārīm* in v. 21 are a different group ('courtiers') from the *śārīm* in vv. 11ff. ('statesmen') is one which should be rejected. And when Weiser says that the prophetic point of view emerges clearly in v. 24, where Baruch passes judgment on the reaction of the king and *all* his officials to the reading of the scroll, this must mean that

[1] B. Duhm, *Das Buch Jeremia* (KHKAT, 1901), *in loc.*
[2] A. Weiser, *Der Prophet Jeremia* (ATD, 1955), *in loc.*
[3] He deletes *kol* before *ʿaḇāḏāw* with G. and says that this is demanded by the contents of v. 25.

the attitude of the officials to the scroll was different from that of Jeremiah, for it cannot be seriously doubted that the *śārīm* of v. 24 include the *śārīm* of vv. 11ff. Hence neither the king nor any of his officials believed in the prophetic word in a way that satisfied Jeremiah. 'They were not afraid and they did not rend their garments.' This applies equally to Elnathan, Delaiah and Gemariah, and the fact that they urged the king not to burn the scroll does not necessarily show that they accepted Jeremiah's *ʿēṣā* as valid and were prepared to respond to it in a way which would have satisfied the prophet.

This conclusion is inescapable unless Duhm's emendation of v. 24 is followed, for the effect of this emendation is to except Elnathan, Delaiah and Gemariah from the adverse judgment passed on the *śārīm* in that verse. It is true that Jeremiah enjoyed the friendship of the family of Shaphan and that Baruch was apparently given the use of Gemariah's *liškā* for the public reading of the scroll,[1] but this adds up to something less than the conclusion that such well-disposed *śārīm* were prepared to concede that the *dāḇār* of a prophet was valid *ʿēṣā* for the conduct of the affairs of a state.

Thus while 36.11ff. and 25 show that certain of the *śārīm* held the prophet in respect and even veneration and had more regard to the sacrosanct character of a prophetic utterance than had the king, they do not show that these *śārīm* approved of this *dāḇār* as a political utterance or believed in it as a political forecast. Consequently the exegesis of 36.16 offered by the commentators cannot stand, because it conflicts with 36.24, which certainly cannot be taken to refer to an entirely different group of *śārīm* from those mentioned in vv. 11ff. Hence the fear experienced by the *śārīm* in the cabinet room did not flow from piety as the commentators suppose, but from deep misgivings about the consequences on the morale of the population of what they must have regarded as a deplorable intervention by Jeremiah.

They had no alternative but to report what amounted to a treasonable speech (vv. 28ff.) to the king and they required precise information as to its source. They interrogated Baruch not in order to ascertain that the words issued from a genuine prophet and so with a view to commending them to the king, but so as to satisfy

[1] See below, p. 122.

themselves that their source was indeed Jeremiah, as they suspected (cf. v. 17). Although he disagreed with them fundamentally as to how the business of a state should be conducted, Jeremiah retained the friendship and respect of certain of the *śārīm* and they were anxious to shield him from the violent reaction which they anticipated from Jehoiakim. It was because of the very serious political estimate which they made of Jeremiah's intervention that they advised Baruch that he and his master should go into hiding forthwith.

It is not my intention to maintain that the behaviour of Jehoiakim and the *śārīm* was totally unrelated to any belief in the potency of the prophetic *dāḇār*. They may have believed in it in the sense in which the devils are said to believe and tremble. It is therefore possible to see in the behaviour of Jehoiakim a kind of religious motivation. The scroll on which Baruch had written Jeremiah's prophecy of the destruction of Judah and Jerusalem was cut in pieces by the king and burned piece by piece (36.20ff.). It is clear that at the time he was incensed against Jeremiah and intended this as an extreme gesture of defiance. But this in itself is a testimony to the importance which he attached to the word of a prophet, since the implication of such an exceptional act of repudiation is that the word of a prophet is a serious utterance whose fulfilment is to be expected.

It may not be extravagant to say that Jehoiakim believed that only by burning the scroll and destroying the prophetic *dāḇār* could he prevent the prediction from working itself out.[1] This, at any rate, is perhaps the point of view of the writer of the chapter and so he records (36.32) that Jeremiah had the scroll rewritten and so, as it were, reinstated the prophecy of doom. As for those *śārīm* who protested against the burning of the scroll, they no doubt were moved by pious scruples and had so much deference and veneration for the word of a prophet[2] as to urge upon the king the unwisdom of such extreme and sacrilegious contumacy. They were unhappy that he should make such an unsavoury theatrical display out of his rejection of the *dāḇār* of a prophet.

This deference is seen on another occasion when Jeremiah had prophesied the destruction of the Jerusalem temple, saying that

[1] On the belief in the potency of the *dāḇār* of a prophet see most recently J. Lindblom, *Prophecy in Ancient Israel*, pp. 53ff.

[2] Cf. J. Lindblom, *ibid.*, p. 203.

Yahweh would make it like Shiloh (26.4–6). The prophets and priests of the Jerusalem temple seized him and threatened him with death (26.8) and the politicians intervened in order to hear the dispute. We are told how they came up from the King's House (where the cabinet room was located according to 36.12) and took their seat in the entry of the New Gate of the house of Yahweh (v. 10).

This is an interesting detail, since we learn from 36.10 that Gemariah, who was one of the *śārīm*, had an office (*liškā*) 'in the upper court at the entry of the New Gate of Yahweh's house'.[1] This is probably to be identified with the *liškā* of the *śārīm* which was located, according to 35.4, above the office of Maaseiah, son of Shallum, 'a keeper of the threshold', i.e. a high temple official.[2] Are we to conclude that this *liškaṯ haśśārīm* was a recognized place for parley between the political and ecclesiastical establishments and that Gemariah, in particular, was a kind of liaison officer? However this may be, it should be noticed that on this occasion the prophets and priests of the Jerusalem temple state their case to the politicians in such a way as to make it appear that it is the security of the state which concerns them and not the defence of their vested ecclesiastical interests. They do not repeat that part of Jeremiah's prophecy of doom which referred specifically to the destruction of the temple (26.11; cf. 26.6).

Jeremiah, for his part, pleads guilty on both counts (26.12), but asserts that this is Yahweh's *dāḇār* and that only repentance can stave off disaster (vv. 12–15). The *śārīm*, who have the well-being of the state in their care, are of necessity greatly perturbed by Jeremiah's words, but they pronounce him not to be worthy of death, because he has spoken in the name of Yahweh (v. 16). That is to say, in any other circumstances his words would have been treasonable, but because he speaks in order to discharge his prophetic responsibility, he enjoys a special immunity. Thus on this occasion the *śārīm* have more respect for the prophetic office than the cultic officers of the Jerusalem temple.

In this the *śārīm* are supported by certain elders who recall that Micah (3.12) had once prophesied destruction against Jerusalem

[1] The use granted to Baruch of this room (36.10) as a kind of pulpit from which he could address the assembled people in the temple court is apparently to be connected with the influence which Jeremiah exerted over the family of Shaphan—a former Secretary of State.

[2] See my note on II Kings 12.10 in *ZAW* 71 (1959), pp. 260–5.

and the temple and that the reaction of Hezekiah and the people of Judah was not anger nor violence but penitence. The elders on whom traditional status and seniority had conferred leadership in the community[1] were therefore recommending that Jeremiah's word should be accepted as Yahweh's verdict and that only the response of penitence and prayer could avert disaster (26.17–19). The elders and the cultic officials were poles apart in their respective attitudes to Jeremiah's word and it is probable that the attitude of the *śārīm* fell somewhere between the two. They were unwilling to silence the prophet, but they could not bring themselves to believe that the prophetic *dāḇār* formed a basis for sound *ʿēṣā*, since they could not reconcile this belief with their political judgment and acumen nor yet with their regard for the public trust reposed in them.

This attitude of respect towards the prophet and even of reliance on his word is affected by Zedekiah, who arranges a secret interview with Jeremiah to discover if he has any further *dāḇār* from Yahweh (37.17). Although the king does what he can to make the prophet's position easier, and to take him out of the hands of the *śārīm* (37.20–21; 38.7–13), it is plain that the latter are now masters of the situation and that Zedekiah, unlike Jehoiakim, has to do what they bid (38.5). For this reason Jeremiah's interview with the king in 38.14ff. is not the momentous occasion it might have been, had Zedekiah been a strong king able to dictate policy. He assures Jeremiah that he will not be put to death for speaking the *dāḇār* of Yahweh, but does not give a firm undertaking in connection with the other point which Jeremiah raises, namely that if he did give *ʿēṣā* to the king, such advice would not be followed (38.15).

Yet Zedekiah is pathetically earnest in his desire to obey the word of Yahweh and weighs seriously Jeremiah's counsel that he should capitulate to the Babylonians and thereby save the city and the royal house from destruction. But he has to beg Jeremiah not to divulge what was said during the interview to the *śārīm* and this underlines the realities of the situation and shows that, even if Zedekiah had been disposed to follow the advice of the prophet, he did not have the power to initiate such a policy.

His attitude, however, certainly proves that he held the word of a prophet in great awe and was prepared to do what he could to

[1] See the discussion on the Ahithophel passage, above, p. 58, n.2.

shield his person from danger and disgrace.[1] In the end he is able to do this only by making Jeremiah a party to subterfuge and by persuading him to give to the *śārīm* what they might well have understood as an undertaking that he had abandoned his purpose of trying to influence the political decisions of the king (38.24–28).

When Jeremiah prophesies the destruction of the state he becomes for those who are responsible for its security an intolerably bad political risk. Yet he has no ulterior motive in this activity; he is concerned only to speak the word of Yahweh and to discharge his duty as a prophet. To do this he has to intervene in politics, for he is a member of Yahweh's 'cabinet' (*sōḏ*) and thus has confidential information concerning Yahweh's *ʿēṣā* which is denied both to statesmen and false prophets. Hence it is said of the false prophets: 'For who (among them) has stood in the *sōḏ* of Yahweh that he should see and hear his word?' (Jer. 23.18). And Amos says: 'Surely Lord Yahweh does nothing except he divulges his *sōḏ* to his servants, the prophets' (3.7). That is, he takes the prophets into his confidence and divulges his policy to them. To be a member of such a 'cabinet' and to have such access to the *dāḇār* of Yahweh is to be better qualified to give *ʿēṣā* concerning the welfare of Judah than any member of a cabinet of *śārīm*.[2]

Yet it is hard for the statesmen to believe this and we have to make an effort to be fair to them, since the account of these matters which is before us is not written from their point of view. They were prepared to tolerate a great deal of what they must have regarded as provocative behaviour on the part of the prophet and we have seen that on one occasion they intervened to save him from the hostility of the cultic officials of the Jerusalem temple and on another connived to hide him from the anticipated fury of Jehoiakim.

The harder attitude of the *śārīm* in chapters 37 and 38 may have

[1] Cf. A. Malamat, 'Jeremiah and the last two Kings of Judah', *PEQ* (1951), pp. 81–87. Malamat argues that from the very outset Zedekiah was a loyal disciple of Jeremiah and that his change of name from Mattaniah to Zedekiah was the result of an utterance of the prophet (23.5–6). Malamat urges that those who regarded Jehoiachin as king *de jure* favoured a Judah-Egypt axis, while the group around Zedekiah and Jeremiah advocated constancy towards Babylon. His explanation of why Zedekiah was ultimately drawn into the rebellion against Babylon is somewhat feeble. He says that this happened not because Zedekiah resiled from his consistent policy of submission to the power which had placed him on the throne but because of his attempt to pacify his personal enemies.

[2] Cf. J. Lindblom, *Prophecy in Ancient Israel*, pp. 112–13.

some connection with the tougher policy of a new Secretary of State (Jonathan in 37.15 and Elishama in 36.20), but it seems principally to have been based on their mistaken conclusion that Jeremiah had attempted to desert to the Babylonians and that he had thereby become a common deserter and deserved the punishment which would be meted out to any traitor (37.11–15). It was intolerable that he should use his prophetic immunity in order to destroy the morale and power of resistance of the soldiers and civilian population of Jerusalem, and what appeared to be an attempt to desert and join those Jews who were already with the Babylonians proved to the satisfaction of the *śārīm* that the intention of his previous speeches had been seditious and that he had had clandestine relations with this treacherous political faction (cf. 38.19, where Zedekiah expresses fear concerning the treatment which might be meted out to him by this dissident group, if he gave himself up to the Babylonians).

The attitude of the *śārīm* is perfectly understandable. Treasonable words allied to what they mistakenly concluded to be treasonable behaviour cannot be tolerated when a city is under siege and is fighting for its life. Not even a prophet can expect immunity if he prophesies pestilence, famine and sword and undermines the common will to resist the enemy by conferring the authority of Yahweh's word on desertion to the Babylonians (38.2). What they might endure from a prophet in a less critical situation they cannot afford to tolerate in a moment of extreme danger. If they had not used force to restrain him, they would have endangered the security of the state and betrayed the public trust which had been placed in them. 'Let this man be put to death . . . for this man is not aiming at the welfare (*šālōm*) of this people but at their harm' (38.4).[1]

[1] In connection with this verse M. Noth, *History*, p. 284, cites the reference in the Lachish Ostraka to those 'who weaken the hands of the land and the city' (vi.6ff.) and remarks: 'If the comment of the writer of the ostrakon does not expressly mention the prophet Jeremiah, it does refer to the influence which proceeded from him and from those who shared his views.' This is a judicious conclusion. Cf. D. W. Thomas, 'The Age of Jeremiah in the Light of Recent Archeological Discovery', p. 2: 'Whether behind the phrase "to weaken the hands" (Ostrakon vi.6) is to be seen a reflection of the activity of the appeasement party which sympathized with Jeremiah in his policy towards the Babylonians must remain uncertain in view of the state of the text at this point.' On the other hand, A. Malamat, 'The Last Wars of the Kingdom of Judah', *JNES* 9 (1950), positively connects this passage with Jer. 38.4–5. Cf. O. Eissfeldt, 'The Prophetic Literature', *The Old Testament and Modern Study* (ed. H. H. Rowley), pp. 152–3.

The statesmen were embarrassed and finally infuriated by Jeremiah's insistence that the most dangerous and delicate matters of state were to be settled in agreement with his *ex cathedra* pronouncements. This was for them a bewildering and unacceptable demand, because Judah was a nation among the nations and it seemed to her statesmen that it was impossible for her to ignore the recognized procedures and universal techniques of international diplomacy. However much they might reverence the prophetic word they could not believe that this was a proper sphere for its unconditional acceptance, and they were convinced that to conclude otherwise was to run away from the realities of the world in which Judah had to engineer her survival into a world of ideal values constructed by prophetic belief to which the real world, with its constant struggle for power among the nations, bore no resemblance.

These men were consequently sincerely convinced that religious faith, even when authorized by the word of a prophet, ought not to decide policy in this sphere. They, too, had a conscience and they were not prepared to concede a demand which seemed to them to hazard the security of the state for which they were responsible.

We are now in a position to state the general theological premisses from which this prophetic intervention into politics derives. From the time that Israel was exposed to the Assyrian menace in the eighth century BC, the old world in which she had existed—a world which had been small and relatively secure—had passed away for ever and she had to confront a perilous and uncertain existence in a much larger world dominated by the struggle for power among the great nations. The prophets inherited from normative Israelite tradition the cardinal belief that history was the theatre of existence where Yahweh revealed himself, and that it was because of his power to shape history to his ends that he was able to lead his people along that historical track which would at length bring them to the place of their destiny.

The prophets did not resile from this traditional article of faith, but they drew out its logic and emphasized certain aspects of it which had hitherto lain somewhat in abeyance. It had been construed as na assertion that history as regulated by Yahweh in relation to his purposes for his people was a *Heilsgeschichte*, but now the prophets discerned in this doctrine not only the promise of salvation but also the threat of judgment, and it was this latter principle of interpretation which seemed to them the more relevant in the new historical situation which was taking shape.[1]

The ultimate threat to Israel was not the military power of Assyria and Babylonia but the threat of Yahweh's judgment. It was Yahweh who was threatening his people and he was simply using the Assyrians and Babylonians to enforce his judgments. The absolute guarantee of security was to be found in trust in Yahweh and compliance with his demands. Acquiescence in these was the condition of historical survival and produced human effort agreeable to the pattern which Yahweh was determined to impose on historical existence. This was what the prophets believed and what the statesmen of Judah found it impossible to believe. When Jeremiah predicted the destruction of Jerusalem as Yahweh's judgment on her sin, the statesmen directed their attention not so much to the prophetic theology on which such a prediction was based as to its disconcerting effects on the morale and security of the state for which they were responsible. For Jeremiah it was a matter of life and death that he should believe in the onset of this judgment, because this was the vindication which was indispensable to him and to those who shared his faith that Yahweh was related to the total movement of history in the manner asserted by the prophets. The impact of judgment on Jerusalem was the proof that Yahweh indeed exercised effective control over history and could make it amenable to his demands.

For the statesmen this activity took on a different colour, because they were not prepared to concede the demands of the prophets. The world as they knew it did not agree with the account of Yahweh's relationship to it given by the prophets. All their experience as practising politicians cried out against the demand that they should surrender their judgment to the revealed word of a prophet. They would have betrayed their own judgment as statesmen and diplomats if they had reposed the security of the state in such a theological assumption or article of faith. They were persuaded that they must continue to rely on those hard-headed, pragmatic procedures which were the general currency of international exchange and that such an intervention as that of Jeremiah

[1] Cf. J. Fichtner, 'Jahves Plan in der Botschaft des Jesaja', pp. 32–33.

in these matters so vital to the security of the state had the effect of weakening Judah's chances of survival in a dangerous world where her fate hung in the balance.[1]

The conflict between prophet and statesman which it has been the purpose of this work to explore is more than an affair of historical interest, for it throws light on a contemporary conflict between the same parties which hinges on the same incompatibilities. If the Israelite prophets were doing no more than raising their voices against certain abuses and were simply seeking to contain wisdom within its proper limits, the theological importance of the conflict would be greatly reduced.

It has been suggested to me that I have misread the nature of the prophetic attack on wisdom and that I ought to have been guided by the analogy of the prophetic criticism of the cult. I do not believe that this analogy is helpful for the present enquiry. In their attack on the *ḥᵃḵāmīm qua* statesmen the prophets are not primarily interested in personalities. They are not saying that the wisdom of statecraft is legitimate, and has merely been abused or perverted by some of its practitioners. If what I have been describing were merely an attack by the prophets on certain individual *ḥᵃḵāmīm* who had an inflated sense of their own importance and were greedy for power, the episode would be of ephemeral interest. But the conflict cannot be described in terms of human deficiencies or excesses. The prophets are not saying to these *ḥᵃḵāmīm* that they are unworthy representatives of their tradition; they are calling in question the basic presuppositions of the tradition itself. This is why the debate has contemporary theological interest.

From the statesman's point of view the prophet does not deal faithfully with the dynamics of historical existence. The debate between the two is fundamentally one about power. The nature of power is complex and difficult to analyse. The prophets are right in insisting that it has spiritual as well as material ingredients and that it is not simply to be equated with economic resources and weight of armament. That political power has subtler elements is, how-

[1] Cf. Jer. 18.18, where the prophet's opponents imply that he engages in subversive activities against both the ecclesiastical and political establishments. 'Come and let us intrigue against Jeremiah, for *tōrā* will not perish from the priest, nor *ʿēṣā* from the *ḥāḵām*, nor *dāḇār* from the prophet.' Here the *ḥāḵām* is the representative of the political establishment and the prophet and priest of the religious establishment and Jeremiah's opponents accuse him of trying to undermine both.

ever, well-understood by statesmen. During the Congo disturbances a British Army officer walked unarmed into an area where there had been pillaging and massacre in order to rescue a number of nuns. In doing this he had to exercise power—real political power—and he did so without any backing of force. He imposed his authority on a lawless and violent situation and brought his mission to a successful conclusion. Here an unarmed soldier exerted more authority on a situation and produced a more positive result than an armed expedition could have done.

But the prophet demands much more than this. His main concern is not that power should be stripped of the fearful crudity and grossness of which it partakes in the awful insecurity of our world—the world of the twentieth century. He does not principally work for the refinement or rarification of power, for this implies gradualism and is a political rather than a prophetic solution. The prophet urges rather that the concept of a balance of power is unreal, because it leaves God out of the reckoning. The Israelite prophets and the contemporary prophets assert that power is not built in with historical existence in the way that the statesmen suppose. God reserves all power to himself and so the *locus* of power is outside historical existence. From this flowed the doctrine of instrumentality in the Israelite prophets. God moves the nations about like pawns on a chess-board, but he is the only real policy-maker and reserves all power to himself.

In this case the statesman ought not to concern himself with power, for, if this is the situation, all that is left for him as for the rest of us is to know the will of God and do it. Beyond this everything rests with God. The statesman will say that the crudity of the balance of power in our world today is a true reflection of the tensions and perilous insecurity of the international community and that it is the unresolved, intractable problems, daunting in their magnitude and delicacy, which will have to be tackled and solved one by one before there is any betterment. But the prophet believes that faith or confidence has a creative potential and can transform a situation. If we had faith in God and loved our neighbour and were prepared to take the absolute risk for the sake of Christ, the world would cease to be an armed camp. So speaks the contemporary Christian prophet.

It is only in this dialectical form that the shape of the relationship between statesman and prophet can be sketched. Otherwise we have to say that the relationship is one of simple incompatibility and to take sides with one or the other. For myself I do not see how the statesman can concede the prophetic demand and continue to be a statesman. If he were to conduct the business of a state on the assumption that the *locus* of power is outside historical existence and is concentrated in God, this would amount to an abdication from political power and responsibility. Certainly it ought not to be supposed that any contribution to the understanding of these matters can be made by the trite observation that we live in a sinful world. We cannot take the myth of the Fall into our analysis of power nor ought we to invoke a moment of eschatological consummation which still lies in the future. We have no grounds for contracting out of the dynamics of historical existence and we should not try to do so either by running back to the Garden of Eden or by yearning for a post-historical Paradise.

INDEX OF AUTHORS

INDEX OF BIBLICAL REFERENCES

Index of Biblical References